HMS *Turbulent*

HMS *Turbulent*

Stephen Wynn

Pen & Sword
MARITIME
AN IMPRINT OF PEN & SWORD BOOKS LTD.
YORKSHIRE - PHILADELPHIA

First published in Great Britain in 2023 by
Pen & Sword Maritime
An imprint of
Pen & Sword Books Ltd
Yorkshire - Philadelphia

ISBN 978 1 52673 626 0

A CIP catalogue record for this book is available from the British Library.

Typeset in INDIA by IMPEC eSolutions
Printed and bound in England by CPI Group (UK) Ltd., Croydon, CR0 4YY

Pen & Sword Books Ltd. incorporates the Imprints of Pen & Sword Archaeology, Atlas, Aviation, Battleground, Discovery, Family History, History, Maritime, Military, Naval, Politics, Railways, Select, Transport, True Crime, Fiction, Frontline Books, Leo Cooper, Praetorian Press, Seaforth Publishing, Wharncliffe and White Owl.

For a complete list of Pen & Sword titles please contact

PEN & SWORD BOOKS LIMITED
47 Church Street, Barnsley, South Yorkshire, S70 2AS, England
E-mail: enquiries@pen-and-sword.co.uk
Website: www.pen-and-sword.co.uk

or

PEN AND SWORD BOOKS
1950 Lawrence Rd, Havertown, PA 19083, USA
E-mail: uspen-and-sword@casematepublishers.com
Website: www.penandswordbooks.com

Contents

Introduction

According to a dictionary entry, the origins of the word turbulent date back to sometime between 1530-40, and come from the Latin word *turbulentus*, meaning restless. It is an adjective, with one of its descriptions being, 'given to acts of violence and aggression'. For HMS *Turbulent*, which served its country so well during the Second World War, it was a very apt description.

There have, in fact, been four other Royal Navy vessels which have carried the name *Turbulent.*

First HMS *Turbulent*

The first Royal Navy vessel to be christened with the name was a wooden-built *Confounder*-class gun-brig. Having been built at Dartmouth in Devon, it was launched on 17 July 1805 under the command of Lieutenant Thomas Osmer.

Although called a gun-brig, it was in essence a sailing vessel, weighing more than 180 tons, measuring 84 feet in length and 22 feet in width, with a crew of fifty officers and ratings. Her armaments included ten 18-pounder cannons, or carronades, along with two 12-pounder guns, making her a formidable attacking force.

On 14 September 1806, *Turbulent* captured the American vessel *Romeo* in the English Channel and sent it in to Dover.

The vessel had been en route from Virginia to Rotterdam at the time it was seized.

An entry in relation to this particular seizure appeared in the *London Gazette* newspaper dated 19 April 1810:

> Notice is hereby given to the Officers and Companies of His Majesty's Gun-Brigs *Turbulent* and *Urgent*, who were actually on board at the capture of the *Romeo*, James Corron, Master, on the 14th Day of September 1806, that they will be paid their respective Proportions of the Net Proceeds thereof, on Wednesday the 2nd May next, between the hours of Eleven and Three, at No. 9, New Bond Street; and all shares not then claimed will be recalled at the same Place every Wednesday and Thursday until the Expiration of Three Months from the first day of payment.

In the early months of 1807, command of *Turbulent* changed hands when Lieutenant Osmer was replaced by Lieutenant John Nops, but this did not prevent it from continuing on as before, because on 4 June 1807, it captured another American schooner, the *Charles*.

Under Nops' command, *Turbulent* went on to capture the American vessel *Mount Etna*, just a matter of days after it had captured the *Charles*, before then capturing the Danish vessel *Providence* the following month.

On 7 September 1807, *Turbulent* was one of the British vessels involved in the capture of the Danish Fleet at Copenhagen. An entry in the *London Gazette* dated 11 July 1809 included the fact that as part of their share of the spoils of war taken from the Danish ships, Petty Officers were awarded

£22 11s 0d, whilst men with the rank of Able Seaman received £3 8s 0d. To provide an idea of the sums involved, £1 in 1806 was worth roughly £92 in 2021, while an average weekly wage for a working man at the time was somewhere in the region of 11 shillings.

In 1808, command of the *Turbulent* became the job of Lieutenant George Wood. During April of that year, Wood and his men captured a total of seven ships in just four days, with four of the vessels being captured on the same day.

On 9 June 1808, during the Napoleonic Wars, a naval conflict was taking place between Denmark-Norway and the British in what has become known as the Gunboat War. On the day in question, *Turbulent* was helping to escort a large merchant convoy consisting of some seventy vessels, when it was attacked by twenty-eight Danish vessels off the island of Saltholm, Denmark. During the battle, *Turbulent* was damaged when it lost its top mast. Although nobody on board the vessel was killed, three of the crew sustained serious injuries before the fighting came to an end after Danish sailors boarded the *Turbulent*, took possession of the vessel, and took her crew as prisoners. The vessel then became part of the Danish navy for the following six years, still sailing under the name *Turbulent*.

Second HMS *Turbulent*

During the First World War, HMS *Turbulent* was a heavily armed *Talisman*-class destroyer. It was one of four that had originally been ordered for the Ottoman navy, initially with the name of *Ogre*, but on 15 February 1915 it was renamed *Turbulent*. It was finally launched on 5 January 1916, but for the British Royal Navy, not the Ottoman navy, and began her service as part of the 10th Destroyer Flotilla of the Grand Fleet on 1 May 1916.

Sadly for *Turbulent* and its crew, it did not survive long. On 1 June 1916, during the Battle of Jutland, the ship was attacked and sunk by the German battleship SMS *Westfallen* during fighting in the early hours of the morning, losing ninety of her crew in the process. The thirteen who survived were captured and taken as prisoners of war.

Third HMS *Turbulent*

Work on the third version of HMS *Turbulent*, an S-class destroyer and one of a batch of sixty-seven such destroyers the Royal Navy ordered in 1917, began on 14 November that year. However, it was not ready for active service until 10 October 1919, nearly two years later.

The third *Turbulent* was a magnificent looking vessel: more than 1,000 tons in weight, 276 feet in length and more than 26 feet in width with a top speed of 36 knots. If those statistics failed to impress, her armaments most definitely would have: two 21-inch torpedo tubes, two 18-inch torpedo tubes, three 4-inch quick-firing guns, and one 2-pounder quick-firing gun (more commonly known as the "pom-pom" anti-aircraft gun).

Despite being nearly 20 years old by the time it became obsolete and broken up in 1936, the ship had seen very little in the way of active service.

Fourth HMS *Turbulent*

The fourth Royal Navy vessel to bear the name *Turbulent*, the subject of this book, was a T-class submarine. Commissioned on 2 December 1941 and first launched in May earlier that year, it was responsible for the sinking of more than 90,000 tonnes of enemy shipping. Her commander, John Wallace Linton DSO DSC RN, was posthumously awarded the Victoria Cross in recognition of this achievement, and the gallantry of *Turbulent's* crew.

Having failed to reply to any further radio messages after 12 March 1943, the submarine then subsequently failed to return to Algiers as expected on 23 March, at the end of its patrol of the Tyrrhenian Sea, after which time it was assumed lost. The full story of this incarnation of *Turbulent* will be covered within the following chapters of this book.

Fifth HMS *Turbulent*

The fifth and final Royal Navy vessel to bear the name *Turbulent* was a *Trafalgar*-class submarine launched in 1982. Its home during its thirty years of service was His Majesty's Naval Base, Devenport. Most of its time was spent gathering military intelligence, although in 2003 it took part in the Allied invasion of Iraq, deploying cruise missiles on more than one occasion.

In 2011 it was part of Britain's military contribution to the NATO-led coalition intervention in Libya, under the terms of the United Nations Security Council Resolution, 1973.

CHAPTER ONE

A Brief History of Submarines

Submarine (noun): a warship with a streamlined hull designed to operate completely submerged in the sea for long periods, equipped with a periscope and typically armed with torpedoes or missiles.

Submarines have been around for hundreds of years, although perhaps not exactly in the way we would consider something a submarine by today's standards. Historical documents make mention of a diving bell used by Alexander the Great (356–323BCE) to carry out reconnaissance missions against his enemies, but the origins of today's submarines can be traced from the late sixteenth century.

Written material from the 1560s includes vessel designs from individuals such as Englishman William Bourne, a noted mathematician of his time, who earlier in his life had been a Royal Navy gunner. However, it was Dutch engineer Cornelis Jacobszoon Drebbel, who had been in the service of the English kings James I (1603–1625) and Charles I (1625–1649), who actually built the first navigable submarine, propelled by oars, in 1620. An updated version of Drebbel's submarine was tested on the River Thames in 1624.

In 1651, the Dutch poet and composer Constantijn Huygens, recorded the following description of one of those tests in his autobiography:

> Worth all the rest put together is the little ship, in which he calmly dived under the water, while he kept the King and several thousand Londoners in the greatest suspense. The great majority of these already thought the man who had very cleverly remained invisible to them, for three hours, as rumour has it, had perished, when he suddenly rose to the surface a considerable distance from where he had dived down, bringing with him the several companions of his dangerous adventure to witness to the fact that they had experienced no trouble or fear under the water, but had sat on the bottom, when they so desired, and had ascended when they wished to do so; that they had sailed whithersoever they had a mind, rising as much nearer the surface or again diving as much deeper as it pleased them to do, without even being deprived of light, yea, even that they had done in the belly of the whale all the things people are used to do in the air, and this without any trouble.
>
> From all this it is not hard to imagine what would be the usefulness of this bold invention in time of war, if in this manner (a thing which I have repeatedly heard Drebbel assert) enemy ships lying safely at anchor could be secretly attacked and sunk unexpectedly utilizing a battering ram, an instrument of which hideous use is made now-a-days in the capturing of the gates and bridges of towns.

More than 100 years later, in 1775, an American by the name of David Bushnell, who had been a teacher, doctor and a combat engineer, designed and constructed the *Turtle*; the world's first purpose-built, military submarine, with enough room for just one man. Indeed, the best way to describe it would be a giant, mis-shaped wine cask, or barrel. It was actually used in a military sense during the American Revolution (1776–1783) and could be submerged, manoeuvred, maintain an air supply and used to attack enemy surface vessels.

It cannot be emphasised enough just how ground breaking Bushnell's invention was. It had a breathing apparatus, which for the man inside it was essential. It used the very water it manoeuvred through as ballast to keep it in an upright position, and, maybe most importantly of all, it had the ability to attach a mine to the hull of an enemy ship, but with sufficient time for the submarine to move to a safe distance before it detonated. It was also possible to remain under water for thirty minutes before needing to return to the surface to replenish the air supply.

Although the *Turtle* was deployed in a military sense, for a number of reasons it achieved no successes against enemy shipping, and was actually sunk by enemy fire whilst on board its transport vessel on 9 October 1776. It was subsequently recovered from the seabed, but was never used for military purposes again. Without a doubt *Turtle* was the first ever vessel that could truly be called a submarine, and if anything, Bushnell and the *Turtle* were simply ahead of their time.

Everything which followed in the future development of submarines can be traced back to September 1776 and the *Turtle's* deployment in the early days of the American Revolution.

The next big breakthrough in submarine use and design was made ninety years later during the American Civil War

(1861–1865). The Confederate Navy, or to use its official title, Confederate States of America, Navy Department, had a submarine called the *H.L. Hunley*, named after its inventor, Horace Lawson Hunley, a marine engineer.

The *Hunley* had an extremely interesting, if somewhat short, military life. Having been built in Mobile, Alabama, it was launched in July 1863, just over two years into the war. The vessel was then moved by rail to Charleston, South Carolina, a distance of more than 600 miles. On its arrival, the *Hunley* was put through its paces and underwent what today would be referred to as "sea trials". Unfortunately, things did not quite go according to plan. The submarine sank during one of its trials, and five Confederate sailors on board were killed. Unperturbed by this failure, the *Hunley* was raised by the Confederates, repaired, and relaunched, but sank again just six weeks later, on 15 October 1863, whilst once again undergoing sea trials. On this occasion, eight members of its crew were lost, including its inventor, Horace Lawson Hunley, who was on board as a civilian observer to see at first-hand how his invention held up. Once again, the *Hunley* was raised from the seabed and put back into service.

On the night of 17 February 1864, the *Hunley* found itself part of the Confederate war machine when it was deployed to attack the 1,260-ton, wooden-hulled Union sloop, the USS *Housatonic*, which was at anchor about 5 miles outside of Charleston harbour as part of the Union's naval blockade of the city.

The *Hunley*, 40 feet in length and 4 feet in width at its widest point, had a crew of eight, every one of them a volunteer, under the command of Lieutenant George E. Dixon. At the front end of the submarine was a 16-foot-long metal spar, and at the front of that was a torpedo filled with 135 lbs of black powder and fitted with a pressure sensitive trigger.

Lieutenant Dixon rammed his torpedo into the wooden hull of the *Housatonic*, the explosion killing five of the ship's crew, which then sank almost immediately, killing the rest of the crew in the process. Although still intact, the *Hunley* also sank, killing all eight members of its crew. Nevertheless, this was the first occasion where a submarine sank a surface vessel.

The *Hunley* is often referred to when the early history of submarines is being discussed. However, the Confederate Navy had carried out previous attacks, albeit unsuccessful ones, with the CSS *David*, although technically speaking the *David* was a submersible and not a submarine.

Built in Charleston in 1863, the CSS *David* was not originally built as a military vessel but as a private venture by local engineering company, T. Stoney. Nevertheless, after coming to the attention of the Confederate Navy, it was put under their control. Similar to the *Hunley,* it had a spar attachment connected to the front of the vessel, on the tip of which was an explosive charge of gunpowder weighing 134 lbs. The *David* had been designed as a submersible, in that although it looked like a submarine, it was technically a surface vessel.

On the evening of 5 October 1863, the *David* slowly made its way out of Charleston harbour under the blanket of darkness and the command of Lieutenant William T. Glassell. Its mission was to attack the USS *New Ironsides*, one of the Union vessels that had been involved in blockading Charleston harbour. The *David* was spotted by the crew of the *New Ironsides* as it drew near, and shots were exchanged between the two vessels. The *David* managed to detonate its torpedo against the hull of the Union vessel, with the subsequent plume of water caused by the explosion landing on top of the *David*, extinguishing its coal fuelled boilers in the process and causing the engine to stop; literarily making it "dead in the water".

Even though the "torpedo" exploded on contact with the hull of the USS *New Ironsides*, it caused very little in the way of damage, and certainly did not even come close to penetrating the ship's hull. With what is known now about blast trauma, it is fortunate that the crew of the *David* were not killed themselves.

The Confederate authorities were not perturbed by this incident, as the *David* carried out at least two other similar attacks in March and April 1864 against the USS *Memphis* and the USS *Wabash*, both of which were unsuccessful.

On 16 April 1863, a French submarine with a twelve-man crew, the *Plongeur* (French for "diver"), was launched. What made the *Plongeur* unique was that it was the first submarine to be propelled by mechanical power using "a compressed-air engine that was propelled by stored compressed air powering a reciprocating engine". The downside of this was that to cater for so much air, the tanks it was stored in took up a large area of the submarine. This was the main reason why, at 146 feet in length, the submarine had to be so long. Yet despite this it could still only manage a speed of about 5 miles per hour.

One of the other differences between the *Plongeur* and its predecessors was that the ram at the nose of the vessel was there to punch a hole through the hull of an enemy ship, before a torpedo was then fired in through the same hole.

In May 1866, the inventor and engineer Julius H. Kroehl, a German American, tested the proficiency of his submarine the *Explorer* at Brooklyn Naval Yard in New York. It was the first submarine able to dive and spend time underwater before returning to the surface and could be controlled by its own crew with no assistance from a surface vessel.

The big change in the usefulness of submarines for military purposes came about in 1866, as a result of Robert Whitehead, an English engineer who came up with the first self-propelled torpedo. The original idea of developing such a weapon had come from Italian engineer Giovanni Lupis, but his idea had a torpedo that was powered by a spring-driven clockwork mechanism.

The torpedo Whitehead wanted to build required an engine, which was provided in the form of a three-cylinder compressed-air engine by the British engineer, Peter Brotherhood. However, it would take a further two years before all of Whitehead's hard work came to fruition and he was able to produce not one, but two torpedoes for the world's navies to marvel at. The bigger of the two was 14 feet in length and carried a 60-pound warhead, with the other being 11 feet with a 40-pound warhead.

The Whitehead torpedo was so unlike anything that had come before it that it became a much sought-after item by navies from around the world. One of these was the British Royal Navy, who in 1871 bought the rights to be able to manufacture the torpedo, although it would take more than thirty years before one was deployed on a Royal Navy submarine, HMS *Holland I*, in September 1902, as part of the First Submarine Flotilla.

The *Holland I* was named after its inventor John Philip Holland, an Irishman from Liscannor in County Clare, who emigrated to America in 1873 when he was 32. As a young man growing up in Ireland, he had worked as both a teacher and an engineer, and once in America he had continued with his engineering, particularly in the arena of submarine design.

By 1875 he had been in discussion with senior figures from the United States Navy with a view to them taking up his ideas. For whatever reason they were not impressed enough to take the matter any further, yet despite this rejection, Holland was not put off and continued to come up with further designs for submarines which he presented to the United States Navy, but once again he met with similar rejection.

In 1900, twenty-five years after he had first submitted submarine designs, he finally had one accepted. On 17 May 1897, Holland launched a submarine with the name *Holland VI.* What was different about this one was it had the ability to run submerged by combining the use of electric motors, which were needed for the submarine to operate under water, along with fuel-driven engines that allowed it to travel on the surface like a normal sea going vessel.

After speaking with Holland in some detail and seeing the *Holland VI* being put through its paces, the United States purchased the submarine on 11 April 1900. After a further six months of sea trials, the vessel was finally commissioned as the USS *Holland* on 12 October 1900, with a further seven more being ordered over the following years. Over time the design was updated with both *Holland I* and *Holland II* types being produced.

The Royal Navy's *Holland I* type submarine, which came into service in 1902, survives to this day at the submarine museum in Gosport, Hampshire. The *Holland I* had a crew of eight and one torpedo tube, whilst the maximum number of torpedoes that could be carried was three. The navies of the world quickly began to realise that as submarine design improved and advanced, so was there a need for the same rate of development of torpedoes. The reality being that without torpedoes, submarines served no real significant military purpose.

During the Russo-Japanese War of 1904–1905, Russia deployed seven of the original Holland-class submarines, which allowed them to have the first ever operational submarine fleet. Due to their newer and more powerful engines, they were able to stay out on patrol, both on the surface and submerged, for more than a day at a time.

Submarine design had progressed so much that by the outbreak of the First World War in 1914, the Royal Navy had a total of eighty different types of submarines. One of these was the D-class, which weighed up to 600 tons, and could travel at a speed of up to 15 knots on the surface and at a maximum of 10 knots when submerged. They had three 18-inch torpedo tubes, a 12-pounder gun mounted at the front of the submarine, and a crew of twenty officers and men.

During the First World War, the Imperial German Navy had a total of 351 submarines, or U-boats, of which a total of 217 were lost along with the lives of 6,000 of their submariners. At the outbreak of the war, Germany only had twenty operational submarines at its disposal, so when measured against the number it had throughout the war, it is easy to see the level of importance it placed on submarines and their potential military effectiveness. By the end of the war, German U-boats had sunk more than 5,000 Allied vessels.

The Royal Navy's best operational submarines were the steam-propelled K-class, sometimes referred to as the "Kalamity" class. Of the eighteen that were built, six were sunk, but none of these were down to enemy action, but simply to accidents. Sadly, with these sinkings also came a number of deaths of British sailors.

An article in the *Leicester Chronicle* dated Friday, 26 May 1967 provides an excellent insight into life on board a K-class submarine.

Killer sub survivor say 'K-boats were jinxed'.

George Kimbell was a qualified signalman on board a K-class submarine. Photographs of the K-class submarines are rare, mainly because they were very much in the "hush-hush" category.

The steam driven submarines were derided by many at the time as impracticable. By an ironic twist of fate, todays Polaris subs, like HMS *Renown*, use their nuclear units to generate heat for steam driven turbines.

On 31 January next year, a 73-year-old Glenfield man will quietly think back to the day, exactly 50 years ago, when he came as near to death as anyone who has yet survived and lived to tell the tale. It is a moment he has relived a hundred times in his imagination since, for the terror of it is unforgiveable.

The man is Mr George Kimbell, now living a peaceful retired life at 59 Triumph Road, Glenfield, far from the indifferent waves which once nearly closed over him for good. On 31 January 1918, he was a qualified signalman serving in HM submarine *K17*, one of the new class "hush-hush" subs, about which many strange stories were then being told, unofficially. There were rumours the boats were killers, jinxed, hoodooed. Officially it was admitted, trouble had been experienced with them on trials.

This was not altogether unexpected. The submarines were steam driven, and had funnels just like a ship for surface cruising. Watertight covers were intended to close over the spot where the funnels, retracted for diving, had been.

The whole diving procedure was complicated, some said too complicated, when compared to that for conventional subs. Too many operations had to be carried out manually, all with the kind of precision timing nowadays expected only of machines. Basically, the boats were ahead of their time. Correct in overall concept (today's nuclear subs are steam-driven), the K boats were let down in their detail design.

All this was so much vague rumour on the night that *K17* got ready to put to sea from Rosyth, along with other boats of the flotilla.

Despite a nagging sickness, which he reported to the Coxswain, George Kimbell remained on duty. Later, the First Lieutenant gave him some medicine and advised him to rest as much as possible. George took to his bunk.

"The time was then around (1530 hours)," he recollects. "I kept having to traverse the boat to reach the toilet. To get there I had to walk cautiously along the narrow passage that ran fore and aft alongside the boiler room. The passageway was long and narrow. The boilers weren't visible, but one side of the passage was very hot and it played havoc with me, the more so for not being very well. The engine room was at the end of this passage.

"I got back to my bunk and had a little sleep. By what I could hear we were leaving harbour in the new order of proceeding out of harbour in darkness. It took a long time to get into order, and when the first watch duty man relieved at 8pm, my colleagues, whose bunks were close to mine, told me briefly how things were going on in the conning tower with my colleague cooper."

Before settling down for the night in his bunk, George decided on one more visit to the toilet, which meant another journey to the other end of the boat, and some good hearted banter with anyone whom he happened to bump into along the way, as by now his toiletry requirements had become common knowledge amongst the rest of the crew.

"I retraced my way back along the passage. I could move only slowly and had not gone more than half way when there was an awful crashing noise somewhere forward. The lights went out and I heard the order, 'Close all watertight doors'. I heard the after door of the passage close and clip. It was the worst moment of my life. I could hear the water rushing in forward. Knowing it was useless to go further, I managed to reach the after door. Being reasonably alert I knew that close by this door there should be a heavy spanner on the bulkhead. I found it and got it down to hit the floor.

"A voice called, 'Who is it?'

"I cried 'I am trapped'. They hurriedly got the door open and realised there was trouble forward. As best I could I told them of the rushing water somewhere in the control room. They shut the door again, and I remember that all communications were dead, the electricity was off, we did for some reason, still have a little lighting in our compartment.

"Escape from the engine room seemed remote, but by the method suggested by the engineers, there was a possible chance, provided we were not under the water, and that of course, we didn't know. We all felt somehow that we were on the surface. Our method of escape was to release all the air in the compartment. There would be a good pressure as more air was stored in groups of long steel bottles.

"The clips were knocked off the engine room hatch cover, and the air kept the water out. To get out, each one climbed on to an iron ladder, and the pressure shot us out. I went about third. As far as I remember we all got out of the engine room, but being dark and with the boat sinking fast by the bow, all seemed cries and confusion."

The fear and confusion that George and his colleagues experienced must have been horrendous. Trying to focus and concentrate on the task at hand whilst knowing that the submarine they were on was taking on water could not have been easy and must have taken great mental strength.

Submarines initially relied on diesel engines which allowed them to travel faster on the surface than underwater. To counter this disability, electric motors powered by batteries were used, although these required recharging, a process only possible when the submarine was on the surface, which also allowed the dumping of the build-up of excess diesel fumes whilst the submarine was submerged.

A submarine's main weapon was, of course, its torpedoes, which was as dangerous a weapon as it was possible to have. These "missiles" weighed up to 3,000 lbs, including somewhere in the region of 500 lbs of high explosives, which, when fired, made their way towards their intended targets causing a large element of fear and trepidation for the crews of the vessels they were attacking. The torpedoes were propelled through the water and directed towards the opposing vessel by a gyro system. When this system failed, it put the crew of the submarine it had been fired from in danger, because in such a situation the torpedo chose its own path, as well as its final destination. In most cases detonation took place when the torpedo struck the hull of the vessel it had been fired at.

It was during the Second World War, in January 1943, when Royal Navy submarines changed from being referred to by a number to a name. It is believed that the man behind this change was Prime Minister Winston Churchill, but Admiral David Richard Beatty is known to have once said, "Submarines should have names as there can be little loyalty to a number".

During the Second World War, the Royal Navy lost a total of forty-five submarines in the Mediterranean, the worst year being 1942, when thirteen submarines were lost. Indeed, the waters of the Mediterranean saw the heaviest submarine losses for the Royal Navy throughout the seven years of the war. Operations in the Far East saw the loss of five submarines, the Atlantic Ocean also saw just five such losses.

CHAPTER TWO

HMS *Turbulent*

HMS *Turbulent* was a T-Class submarine ordered by the Admiralty from the ship builders Vickers Armstrong, of Barrow-in-Furness, on 4 September 1939, the day after Britain declared war on Nazi Germany.

The T-class, or *Triton*-class, of submarine first came into service in 1934, specifically to replace the *Odin* (O-class), the *Parthian* (P-class), and the *Rainbow* (R-class) submarines, which had been the Royal Navy's boats of choice throughout the 1920s and 1930s. None of these, it has to be said, had really lived up to what had been expected of them, due in no small part to the fact that they were all mechanically unreliable and slow, traits that were not particularly good for any type of military vessel, especially in a time of war.

Before looking at *Turbulent's* relatively short service history in more detail, it is useful to take a brief look at the development of submarine design throughout the 1920s and 1930s. Three main agreements provided a framework for the development in submarine warfare. These were the Washington Naval Agreement (1922); the London Naval Agreement (1930), and the London Disarmament Conference (1935/6).

The conference surrounding the Washington Naval Agreement took place at the Memorial Continental Hall, Washington, beginning in November 1921 and finishing on 6 February 1922. The agreement was signed by the governments of France, Great Britain, Italy, Japan and the United States of America; in essence the victorious nations of the First World War. The idea for the conference was to limit the number of naval vessels each country was allowed to build and maintain. For some strange reason this did not include cruisers, destroyers or submarines. However, the treaty did say that each country's submarines should be retired after a period of thirteen years. This meant that in order to keep to the terms of the agreement, the Royal Navy's *Oberon*-class submarines would have to be taken out of service by August 1940. However, due to the outbreak of the Second World War, this did not happen.

Despite agreements having been reached in February 1922, the treaty was not ratified until August 1923, and it was then not logged with the League of Nations until 16 April 1924, a process which appears to have been painfully slow.

The official title of the London Naval Agreement was the International Treaty for the Limitation of Naval Armament, and the countries who took part in the one-day conference in London on 22 April 1930 were the same attendees and signatories to the Washington Naval Agreement of 1922. This in turn was ratified on 27 October 1930, becoming effective immediately, and logged with the League of Nations on 6 February 1931.

The 1930 agreement regulated submarine warfare, cruisers and destroyers, and agreed the level of naval ship building each country was allowed to undertake. For five countries who had been allies in the First World War to have to come to such an agreement in the first place seems slightly strange, although at the outbreak of the war, Italy had been a partner in the Triple Alliance with Germany and Austria-Hungary. Rather than go to war, Italy decided to remain neutral and, on 26 April 1915, signed the Pact of London with Britain and France, resigned from the Triple Alliance on 3 May, and declared war on Austria-Hungary on 23 May.

The following Articles of the Treaty specifically related to submarines.

Part II, Article 6, Section 2

The standard displacement of a submarine is the surface displacement of the vessel complete (exclusive of the water in non-watertight structure) fully manned, engine and equipped ready for sea, including all armament and ammunition, equipment, outfit, provisions for crew, miscellaneous stores, and implements of every description that are intended to be carried in war, but without fuel, lubricating oil, fresh water or ballast water of any kind on board.

Part II, Article 7, Section 1

No submarines the standard displacement of which exceeds 2,000 tons (2,032 metric tons) or with a gun above 5.1 inch (130 mm) calibre shall be acquired by or constructed by or for any of the High Contracting Parties.

Section 2

Each of the High Contracting Parties may however, retain, build or acquire a maximum number of three submarines of a standard displacement not exceeding 2,800 tons (2,845 metric tons); these submarines may carry guns not above 6.1 inch (155 mm) calibre. Within this number, France may retain one unit already launched, of 2,880 tons (2,926 metric tons), with guns the calibre of which is 8 inches (203 mm).

Section 3

The High Contracting Parties may retain the submarines which they possessed on 1 April 1930 having a standard displacement not in excess of 2,000 tons (2,032 metric tons) and armed with guns above 5.1 inch (130 mm) calibre.

Section 4

As from the coming into force of the present treaty in respect of all the High Contracting Parties, no submarine the standard displacement of which exceeds 2,000 tons (2,032 metric tons) or with a gun above 5.1 inch (130 mm) calibre shall be constructed within the jurisdiction of any of the High Contracting Parties, except as provided in paragraph 2 of this Article.

Part IV, Article 22

The following are accepted as established rules of international rules.

Section 1

In their action with regard to merchant ships, submarines must confirm to the rules of International Law to which surface vessels are subject.

Section 2

> In particular, except in the case of persistent refusal to stop on being duly summonsed, or active resistance to visit or search, a warship, whether surface vessel or submarine, may not sink or render incapable of navigation a merchant vessel without having first placed passengers, crew and ships papers in a place of safety. For this purpose, the ship's boats are not regarded as a place of safety unless the safety of the passengers and crew is assured, in the existing sea and weather conditions, by the proximity of land, or the presence of another vessel which is in a position to take them on board.

In a practical sense this was never going to be workable. There was absolutely no way a submarine who had come across an escorted convoy, comprising merchant vessels, was ever going to comply with this aspect of international law, as it would have meant certain death to have surfaced anywhere nearby. A number of the vessels which HMS *Turbulent* would later sink, or attack without warning, were unarmed merchant vessels. These included the *Sangini, Delia, Rosa M,* and the *Constantino Borsini.*

Such restrictions placed on attacking vessels as to how they should conduct themselves when dealing with merchant vessels might well have appeared quite impressive amongst the pages of a multi-nation signed treaty, but how was that ever conceivably going to work in a practical sense if not all nations were prepared to sign it?

The London Naval Disarmament Conference of 1935-36, also referred to as the Second London Naval Treaty, was a very interesting affair, although it would be fair to say that it was the least successful and effective of the three conferences.

Lasting for more than three months between 9 December 1935 and 25 March 1936, the treaty was eventually signed by Australia, Canada, France, India, New Zealand, the United Kingdom and the United States. South Africa refused to sign, as did the Irish Free State, the latter simply because it did not have or maintain a navy. Japan withdrew from the conference on 15 January 1936 as at the time it was at war with China. Another country who did not sign the treaty was Italy, which had been at war with Ethiopia since October 1935, resulting in the League of Nations placing it under sanctions.

The main point of the conference was to limit countries from increasing the size of their navies. Japan's decision to withdraw from the conference meant that trying to effectively introduce and implement anything useful had been made a whole lot harder. Only three countries signed the treaty; France, the United Kingdom and the United States, so in many respects it could be deemed that whatever actually came out of the conference was pointless.

In relation to submarines, it was agreed by the treaty's signatories that there would be a limit to their size, with no one submarine weighing more than 2,000 tons, and having no deck guns bigger than 5.1 inches. Taking into account that the Royal Navy's T-class submarines, such as *Turbulent,* weighed in at 1,290 tons when on the surface, and were 276 feet 6 inches in length, they were formidable sized boats. Axis submarines were of varying sizes, but it was *Turbulent's* overall size and ability to manoeuvre at speed that ultimately made it so impressive. Somewhat ironically, Britain already had submarines that weighed in at around 2,000 tons in the form of the old K-class submarines, although, as we have seen, they had proved somewhat unreliable, which would have no doubt been known to her allies. This in turn begs the question why it was felt necessary to restrict submarines to 2,000 tons.

An aspect of the treaty that is somewhat confusing is the genuinely held belief at the time that it was a qualified success, being seen in some quarters as an important contribution to world peace. With Germany and Japan being unprepared or unwilling to be a signatory, it is unclear how anybody could have ever seriously held such a belief. After Adolf Hitler was appointed chancellor of Germany on 30 January 1933, the country ultimately changed from being a democracy to a dictatorship. In less than one month of coming to power, laws were enacted that reduced the civil rights of the German people. Perhaps the most dangerous piece of legislation Hitler had at his disposal was the 'Enabling Act', agreed by the Reichstag on 23 March 1933, which allowed him to enact new laws without the agreement of either President Hindenburg or the Reichstag for a period of four years.

Meanwhile, Japan had been a signatory of the London Naval Treaty in 1930, but the following year had invaded and conquered Manchuria. On 15 May 1932, the Japanese Prime Minister, Inukai Tsuyoshi, was assassinated, allowing the nation's military to assert an increasing influence over the country, and in 1933 there was international condemnation concerning the occupation of Manchuria, which ultimately resulted in Japan withdrawing from the League of Nations.

One positive aspect to come out of the treaty was that it confirmed Article 22 of the 1930 agreement. All the world's major powers were invited to express their agreement to the rules embodied by Article 22, which became known as the London Submarine Protocol. More than thirty-five nations eventually subscribed to it, including the U.S., Great Britain, Germany, and Japan. With the Second World War beginning just three years later, it was a short-lived agreement.

The following two points of Article 22 became accepted as established rules of international law:

> (1). In their action with regard to merchant ships, submarines must conform to rules of international law to which surface vessels are subject.
>
> (2). In particular, except in the case of persistent refusal to stop on being duly summoned, or of active resistance to visit or search, a warship, whether surface vessel or submarine, may not sink or render incapable of navigation a merchant vessel without having first placed passengers, crew and ship's papers in a place of safety. For this purpose the ship's boats are not regarded as a place of safety unless the safety of the passengers and crew is assured, in the existing sea and weather conditions, by the proximity of land, or the presence of another vessel which is in a position to take them on board.

Although at first glance this might not appear to have any real significance, it was used at the post-war trial of the man who took over from Adolf Hitler as the German head of state in 1945, Karl Donitz, who issued the instruction to his U-boats to construct a policy of unrestricted submarine warfare. At his Nuremberg war crimes trial, he was found guilty of having committed crimes against humanity, crimes against peace, and war crimes against the laws of war. Not only did he survive the hangman's noose, he only received a ten-year prison sentence.

HMS *Turbulent* (N98)

HMS *Turbulent* was launched on 12 May 1941 at the Vickers Armstrong shipyard at Barrow-in-Furness. On 30 November of that year it left the yard and headed for Holy Loch, north-west of Glasgow, before being commissioned on 2 December 1941. After its arrival *Turbulent* conducted a number of speed trials and took part in training exercises until 9 December, after which time it moved on to Arrochar, a village located near the head of Loch Long. There *Turbulent* underwent its torpedo discharge trials, which lasted for the next six days, before returning to Holy Loch to undertake more training exercises in the Clyde area. It remained there until 3 January 1942, when it departed for Gibraltar with HMS *Tempest*. The two submarines were escorted to Bishop Rock by the minesweeper HMS *La Capricieuse*. *Turbulent*'s first patrol, to the Alboran Sea, just to the east of Gibraltar, only lasted a week and it returned to Gibraltar on 21 January.

Turbulent next left Gibraltar on 27 January and took part in anti-submarine exercises with the *Egret*-class sloop HMS *Pelican*, and the two *Flower*-class corvettes, HMS *Azalea* and HMS *Marigold*.

After completing the exercise *Turbulent* arrived at Malta on 2 February, before beginning its second war patrol just two days later, with instructions to cover the area of Suda Bay, Crete, before making its way to its new base at Alexandria as part of the 1st Submarine Flotilla. Having spent only a week at sea, *Turbulent* returned to base on 13 February.

HMS *Turbulent's* reign of terror in the Mediterranean began on the afternoon of 27 February 1942, when the British submarine was on patrol in the seas off Monemvasia, in Greece. It came across the Greek caique, or schooner, the

Agios Charalambos, which at 60 tons was not a particularly big vessel, but as it appeared to have a large cargo strapped to its deck, *Turbulent*'s captain, Commander John Linton, obviously considered it to be a worthwhile target to engage. Maybe because of the relatively small size of the vessel, Linton decided rather than use up one of his valuable torpedoes, he would surface and use his deck gun to sink the vessel instead.

Another Greek vessel, the *Evangelista*, was a small, 45-ton, two-masted sailing vessel, and in the early afternoon of 2 March 1942, was sailing in the waters of the Kassandra peninsula, off the Greek coast. As had been the case previously when attacking similar sized enemy shipping, Linton had chosen not to use any of his torpedoes, but instead chose to surface and engage the enemy with his deck gun. A number of the rounds fired by *Turbulent* struck the *Evangelista*, causing it to sink in less than half an hour.

About forty minutes later, *Turbulent* came across another Greek schooner. This time it was the 250-ton *Aghios Apostolos*. Once again, Linton decided to surface and utilise his deck gun rather than use up any of his torpedoes. Several shots struck the Greek vessel and although it did not sink, it was badly damaged, with three of the shots striking below the water line. The *Aghios Apostolos* made its way towards land before eventually beaching on rocks.

Turbulent's day was not yet over, and good fortune once again came its way. As was normal procedure, during the hours of darkness Linton kept his boat on the surface. After sailing like this for about three and a half hours, another Greek vessel came in to view. This time it was the two-masted schooner the *Chariklia*. Linton took his time, happy in the knowledge that his intended prey was not aware of his presence in the darkness of the late evening. He closed to within 500 yards before opening fire, and, not surprisingly at that distance, every shot fired struck the target, causing the *Chariklia* to sink in just a matter of minutes.

No sooner had Linton and his crew finished one attack than they spotted yet another Greek ship. This time it was the *Aghios Dionyssios*, a small, masted schooner, just south of the Kassandra peninsula. Once again, *Turbulent* attacked by using its deck gun. The "cargo" on board the *Aghios Dionyssios* on this occasion was German soldiers, a number of whom were killed in the attack.

The relatively small, 24-ton Greek schooner, the *Prodromos*, was attacked by HMS *Turbulent* on the afternoon of 3 March 1942. Not a lot of information is available on this particular vessel, but it is known that there were a number of women on board when it was initially attacked. When this fact was ascertained by Commander Linton, he immediately called off the attack, but not before several women on board had been killed or injured. Why there were such a large number of women on board the *Prodromos*, and what their purpose was, is unclear. The vessel made it to the small island of Skiathos, situated off the east coast of Greece, arriving there the morning after the attack.

Not long after this incident, the *Prodromos* was acquired by the German *Kriegsmarine* and turned in to a motor tanker. The vessel was eventually sunk on 9 May 1944 by units of the Soviet Army.

On 5 March 1942 *Turbulent* was north of the Doro Channel in the Aegean Sea, a strait which separates the Greek islands of Karystos to the north and Tinos to the south, when it came across a small convoy of unknown escorted vessels. Having begun its attack, *Turbulent* fired off four of its torpedoes, but not one of them struck their intended targets. It is not known if the convoy or its escorting vessels ever realised that they had actually been attacked.

The Greek schooner *Agia Paraskevi* was attacked and sunk on 12 March 1942 after *Turbulent* had surfaced and opened fire with its deck gun just north of the Zea Channel. *Turbulent's* gun fire had been extremely accurate, ensuring the demise of the Greek vessel within a matter of minutes.

In the early hours of the following day, 13 March, *Turbulent* saw and attacked another Greek schooner, the *Anastassi*, this time off the coast of Serifos. Having surfaced, it opened fire with its deck gun and caused sufficient damage for the *Anastassi* to capsize initially, before completely sinking beneath the waves.

In the afternoon of 7 April 1942, a week into its fourth war patrol, *Turbulent* spotted the heavily laden Italian merchant vessel *Rosa M*, just south of Petrovac, Croatia, whilst it was on route to Durazzo. Having decided to surface rather than use its torpedoes, *Turbulent* opened fire with its deck gun, striking the *Rosa M* enough times to cause it to sink.

As was commonplace with submarine attacks on surface vessels, not all of them were successful. A number of torpedoes that missed their targets exploded after hitting nothing more substantial than the sand on a beach. This is exactly what happened on 9 April 1942, when HMS *Turbulent* carried out an attack on an Italian merchant vessel, the *Constantino*, off the coast of Croatia, near Sibenik. Two torpedoes were fired and both of them missed.

Commander Linton did not seem to care how large or small an enemy vessel was. The only criteria he seemed driven by was to attack and sink any enemy vessel he came across, regardless of its purpose. On 14 April 1942, and whilst still patrolling in Croatian coastal waters, he attacked and sank a small Italian vessel, the *Franco*. Meanwhile, the *Delia*, an Italian merchant vessel, was sunk after being struck by two torpedoes on 16 April 1942, off the Italian coast near Brindisi.

It was nearly a month before *Turbulent* managed to sink another enemy vessel, although after the end of its previous war patrol on 22 April 1942, it did not return to sea to begin its fifth war patrol until 11 May, with orders to remain in the Gulf of Sirte.

Four days into the patrol, on 14 May 1942, *Turbulent* spotted two Italian sailing vessels off the Libyan coast at Ras el Hilal. It surfaced and engaged one of the vessels with its deck gun. After a number of shots had struck the Italian vessel the *San Guisto*, its crew "abandoned ship" and it ran aground.

Just four days later, in the early hours of 18 May 1942, *Turbulent* was patrolling off the Libyan coast near Benghasi when it spotted an Italian merchant vessel, the *Bolsena*, which was in convoy with another vessel, both of whom were under escort by an Italian naval ship. *Turbulent* fired off three torpedoes, two of which struck the *Bolsena*, causing it to sink in minutes. More than half of the crew of eighty-four were killed.

The *Anna Maria Gualdi* was an Italian merchant ship of just over 3,000 tons, which spent most of its time transporting fuel across the Mediterranean Sea. Late on the evening of 28 May 1942, HMS *Turbulent* spotted two Italian merchant vessels heading south, escorted by two Italian destroyers some miles off the Libyan coast. One of the vessels was the *Anna Maria Gualdi*. A game of cat and mouse took place over a period of more than six hours, which was made extremely difficult because of the heavy mist. Nevertheless, the *Anna Maria Gualdi* and the other Italian destroyer, the *Antonio Pigafetta*, both survived the attack.

On 29 May 1942, the *Capo Arma* was in convoy about 70 miles north-west of Benghazi, Libya, when it was struck and sunk by three torpedoes fired by HMS *Turbulent.*

One of the other vessels with the *Anna Maria Gualdi* at the time of the May attack was the Italian naval destroyer the *Emanuele Pessagno,* which sank when a torpedo fired by *Turbulent* and intended for the *Capo Arma* had a gyro malfunction and struck the Italian destroyer instead.

On 2 June 1942, HMS *Turbulent* attacked the German submarine *U-81* (famous for having attacked and sunk the Royal Navy's aircraft carrier HMS *Ark Royal* on 13 November 1941), under the command of Kapitanleutnant Friedrich Guggenberger, approximately 150 miles off the Egyptian coast. *Turbulent* first caught sight of *U-81* at 1250 hours, and eleven minutes later opened fire with the first of five torpedoes from a distance of 1,500 yards. At 1309 hours, *Turbulent,* now 2,500 yards from *U-81,* opened fire again with two more torpedoes.

Despite firing a total of seven torpedoes, every single one of them missed their intended target. Nevertheless, three loud bangs were heard at the time and wreckage was seen floating on the water's surface soon afterwards. Yet whatever it was, it was most definitely not that of *U-81,* as the submarine remained at large and by the time it was sunk at Pola, Croatia, on 9 January 1944 by US bomber aircraft, it had sunk a total of twenty-six Allied vessels.

On the evening of 23 June 1942, *Turbulent* came very close to being destroyed itself whilst looking for targets to attack. Off in the distance, approximately 5 miles away, Commander Linton spotted two vessels, one of which was a merchant vessel and the other its escort, the Italian torpedo boat, *Perseo.* Within a matter of minutes, *Turbulent* was spotted and suddenly changed from being the predator to the prey.

For more than an hour, Commander Linton and his crew had to endure the trauma of being depth charged by the *Perseo*, but despite one or two of them detonating close by, no serious damage was sustained.

On the morning of 24 June 1942, *Turbulent* was off the coast of Libya, near Ghemines, when it spotted the 1,000-ton Italian merchant vessel, the *Regulus*. Two torpedoes were fired, one of which hit its intended target. To save it from sinking, its crew managed to beach it, although it never sailed again.

On 4 July 1942, the *Ankara*, an Italian merchant vessel, was part of a convoy which also included the *Nino Bixio* and the *Monviso* and was heavily defended by an escort of eight Italian naval vessels. Unbeknown to any of the Axis ships, they were being followed by HMS *Turbulent*, who was waiting for an opportunity to carry out an attack. However, it was ultimately unable to do so because the convoy was so heavily protected. What is not known is whether any, or all, of these merchant vessels were carrying Allied POWs at the time.

HMS *Turbulent* is possibly best known for the attack it carried out on 17 August 1942 on the Italian cargo vessel, the *Nino Bixio*, which at the time was carrying an estimated 3,200 Allied prisoners of war who had been captured during the North African campaign.

The *Nino Bixio* was travelling from Benghazi to Brindisi when it was attacked by HMS *Turbulent*. Two torpedoes fired by *Turbulent* struck the *Nino Bixio* causing severely damage, although not enough to sink it. A total of 336 Allied POWs were killed in the attack, which will be covered in greater detail later in this book.

On 17 August 1942, the same day that *Turbulent* attacked the *Nino Bixio*, it also attacked the Italian merchant vessel, the *Sestriere*, which was also fully laden with Allied POWs. Fortunately for those on board, the two torpedoes fired at the *Sestriere* both missed, meaning that potentially hundreds of Allied POW lives were saved.

The *Kreta* was a 904-ton German cargo ship and the very fact that it was still afloat, let alone being used as part of the German war effort, was truly remarkable, having been built and launched way back in 1866 by Barclay, Curle & Co. Ltd., in Glasgow, Scotland.

It had started out as part of the Leith, Hull & Hamburg Line and began life as the SS *Cumberland*, as it remained until 1919 when it then became the MV *Lisa*, sailing under a Swedish flag. In 1941, it was purchased by the German government and renamed the MV *Kreta*.

On 8 October 1942, the *Kreta* was attacked some 10 miles north of Ras al Hilal, Libya, by HMS *Turbulent*, and was sunk after being struck by a torpedo fired from 1,000 yards. A second torpedo was fired but missed its target.

On the afternoon of 11 November 1942, the MV *Benghazi*, a 1,500-ton German auxiliary submarine tender, was on route from La Spezia to Cagliari, Italy, when it was attacked by HMS *Turbulent* near Cape Ferrato. Out of a crew of eighty-one there were seventy-eight survivors. The vessel was comparatively new, having been built in Denmark in 1933. It had begun life as the MV *Almeria*, before being captured by warships of the Vichy French government in 1940 and becoming the MV *Saint Phillipe*. A year later it was seized by the German *Kriegsmarine* and renamed the MV *Benghazi*.

On its tenth war patrol, HMS *Turbulent* was patrolling off Cape Ferrato, Sardinia, when on 29 December 1942 it spotted the 5,000-ton Italian merchant vessel, the *Marte*. In mid-afternoon and in calm waters, it fired off two of its torpedoes from a distance of just over 1,300 yards. Only one of them struck its intended target, but it was sufficient enough to send the Italian vessel to the sea bed.

With Christmas and New Year celebrations out of the way, not that would have included much for the crew of a submarine on a war patrol in the Mediterranean, *Turbulent* was off the coast of Calabria, Italy, when it spotted the Italian merchant vessel, the *Vittoria Beraldo*. It was the morning of 11 January 1943, the early days of a new year, and the fifth year of the Second World War.

In one and a half hours, the two vessels were involved in a game of hide and seek, which eventually resulted in the demise of the Italian merchant vessel. Having tracked it for about thirty minutes, *Turbulent* fired two torpedoes, both of which missed. This was more to do with the distance between the two vessels and the speed of the torpedoes, as the further away *Turbulent* was when it opened fire, the more time the *Vittoria Beraldo* had to react and take defensive measures.

When Commander Linton realised what had happened, he brought his submarine to the surface and opened fire with his deck gun. Although more successful than the torpedo attack, it was still not sufficient to sink the *Vittoria Beraldo*, and *Turbulent* was forced to dive for its own safety when it came under attack from a shore battery. Unperturbed, Linton ordered that another torpedo be fired, but this also missed. With the bit clearly between his teeth, Linton surfaced again and opened fire with his deck gun. Although none of the rounds struck the *Vittoria Beraldo*, it ran aground at Cetraro whilst the inland batteries focussed their fire on *Turbulent*. Realising the danger he was in, Linton quickly dived the submarine. Under the safety of the water's surface, he took his time to reposition his submarine and fire a single torpedo. Within seconds, the *Vittoria Beraldo* was no more.

Three days later, *Turbulent* finished its tenth war patrol and returned to its base at Malta.

After a break of eleven days, with the crew suitably refreshed and the submarine's supplies and munitions fully replenished, *Turbulent* set sail on its eleventh war patrol.

On 1 February 1943, in the waters off Cape San Vito, Linton spotted the 5,000-ton Italian merchant vessel the *Pozzuoli*, which was heading in the general direction of Palermo. Linton was surprised to see it was unescorted. Hardly able to believe his good fortune, he quickly closed in on his target and when he was less than 1,000 yards away, fired two of his torpedoes. Both struck the ship causing catastrophic damage, sinking it in a short space of time. Four days later, on 5 February 1943, the Italian Merchant tanker SS *Utilitas* was travelling from Taranto to Palermo with a cargo of 5,000 tons of urgently needed fuel when it was attacked and sunk by HMS *Turbulent*.

Commander John Linton was clearly a determined individual. A good example of his single-minded approach to being in charge of a Royal Navy submarine was demonstrated in the sinking of the Italian merchant vessel, the *San Vincenzo*.

On 1 March 1943, Linton spotted his prey off the Italian coast at Paola. He despatched two of his torpedoes in quick succession, but incredibly they both missed. Rather than fire any more of his precious torpedoes and risk missing yet again, he chose to surface and open fire with his deck gun. It is not known how many shots were fired and how many struck the target, but enough of them did and the *San Vincenzo* was sunk.

It is also believed that on 3 March 1943, Linton's submarine was responsible for sinking the Italian sailing vessels the *Gesu*

Giuseppe E Maria and the *Pier Delle Vigne*, which were sailing off the coast of Sicily at the time. Because of *Turbulent's* own demise soon afterwards, it has never been possible to confirm that this was actually the case.

HMS *Turbulent* and its crew was subsequently lost, it is believed, off the coast of Sardinia on 12 March 1943. The circumstances of how it met its end have been a point of discussion ever since. The rumours have varied between claiming it was sunk by a bomb dropped by a German aircraft, it hit a mine, or was sunk by an Italian torpedo boat.

When the loss of a submarine occurred during the Second World War and there was no confirmation of how it had met its end, it was common practice for the British government to attribute the loss of such a vessel to it either having struck a mine, been depth charged, or torpedoed by an enemy submarine or torpedo boat. Its location would be guessed based on the route that the submarine was known to be on and its position at the time of its last radio communication.

What is known is that HMS *Turbulent* left the port of Algiers to begin a patrol off the west coast of Italy. By 3 March 1943 it had attacked and sunk three Italian vessels, but having sent no communication since 12 March, it failed to return to Algiers on 23 March at the end of its patrol, as expected.

A good example of the uncertainty over what happened to HMS *Turbulent*, and where and how it met its end, can be found in an entry from the forum of The Society for Nautical Research, dated 3 November 2008, written by an anonymous guest:

> The well-respected *Jane's Defence Weekly* magazine includes entries for HMS *Turbulent*, the first of which was taken from the 1944–45 edition, in which it states,

> "Turbulent (1941) reported missing (23) March 1943 (depth-charged by It. MA3 off Sardinia)." By the time of the Supplementary War Losses section, which was included in the 1947-48 edition of the magazine, this had changed to, "Turbulent was probably mined off Sardinia, March 23 (14) 1943."

During its relatively short period of service, *Turbulent* was ultimately responsible for the sinking of twenty-one enemy vessels, as well as damaging a number of others, making it one of the most successful British submarines of the Second World War.

CHAPTER THREE

Commander John Wallace Linton VC DSO DSC RN

HMS *Turbulent*'s commander, John Wallace "Tubby" Linton was born in Malpas, Newport, on 15 October 1905, the eldest son to parents Edward Linton, who was a land agent, and Margaret Linton. John's younger brother, Patrick, was born five years later, on 24 October 1910, in Glamorgan.

According to the 1911 Wales Census, the Linton family were living at 35 Stow Park Avenue, Newport, and because of Edward's job, the family was affluent enough to be able to afford to have three servants looking after them.

Having been educated at Osborne, in the Isle of Wight, and at Dartmouth, both of which were Royal Navy colleges, Linton joined the Royal Navy on 15 July 1926, when he was 21 years of age.

Having completed his basic training, Linton found himself briefly serving on board the Royal Navy's *Dragon*-class cruiser HMS *Dauntless*, in the Mediterranean Sea. Launched on 10 April 1918, the ship had not begun its operational service until early 1919.

Being an officer in the Royal Navy did not come easily, and for Linton he underwent his Lieutenant's training course at both Greenwich and Portsmouth naval colleges, where nobody had an "easy ride".

His time as a submariner began on 25 July 1927, the day before he became a Sub-Lieutenant. A reference to this announcement was made in the *London Gazette* on Tuesday, 2 August 1927. He attended the Royal Navy's shore base, HMS Dolphin, at Fort Blockhouse in Gosport, the home of the Royal Navy's Submarine Service. For Linton this was the beginning of a further four months training, which he successfully completed, and on 21 November 1927 was appointed as Third Hand on board HMS *L22.* At 150 feet in length and with a crew of just thirty-eight officers and men, it was a relatively small submarine. Linton only spent five months serving on *L22* before transferring to HMS *Oberon*, which was part of the 5th Submarine Flotilla, on 15 April 1928.

On 27 July 1928, his promotion to the rank of Lieutenant, effective from 15 July, was announced in the *London Gazette.*

Running parallel with his love of the sea and serving in the Royal Navy was his passion for playing rugby union; his short, stocky build making him an ideal candidate as a front row forward. Even today, playing the game in such a position requires an individual to have a particular kind of mindset and mental strength which determines that it is most definitely not a game, or position to play, for those individuals with a delicate constitution.

On 6 April 1929, aged 24, Linton married Nancy Kaye Pitts-Tucker in Luttleworth, Leicestershire, and the couple went on to have two sons: William Francis (1930), and James Anthony (1933).

Just four months after his marriage, Linton transferred to HMS *H43*, which was neither particularly large or fast. At 171 feet in length, weighing 430 tons when on the surface, it had a top speed of 11.5 knots (13.2mph). Its full complement of officers and ratings was just twenty-two men.

The year 1932 brought with it a change of scenery for Linton, as he found himself stationed in Hong Kong as First Lieutenant on board HMS *Oswald*, as part of the 4th Submarine Flotilla. Linton stayed with *Oswald* until December 1934, before returning to the UK to take the Commanding Officer's Qualifying Course, which began on New Year's Eve.

Six years later, on 1 August 1940, HMS *Oswald*, which by then had moved from the Far East to the Mediterranean, was seen by four Italian destroyers whilst running on the surface 15 miles south-east of Cap Spartivento, Italy. Before being able to dive and leave the area, *Oswald* was rammed and sunk by the Italian destroyer *Vivaldi*. Somewhat miraculously, only three members of the crew were killed, with fifty-two managing to survive.

After having successfully completed the Commanding Officer's Qualifying Course, Linton was placed in command of submarine *L21*, part of the 5th Submarine Flotilla, which had been built for the Royal Navy during the latter stages of the First World War. His time in charge of *L21* was short lived. In fact, it was less than three months. On 15 August 1935 he was given command of the S-class submarine HMS *Snapper*, which had only come into service two months earlier.

Snapper and *Turbulent* were not just connected because of John Linton, but because they both went out on patrol and were never heard of again. In *Snapper's* case, it left its base on the River Clyde on 29 January 1941, and went missing the following month.

On 11 May 1936, as part of Linton's on-going training, he saw service on board the Royal Navy's prestigious dreadnought-style battleship HMS *Iron Duke*, so named after Arthur Wellesley, the 1st Duke of Wellington, the victor at Waterloo. In 1930, the ship was demilitarised under the London Naval Treaty as part of the agreement between France, Italy, Japan, the United Kingdom and the United States to reduce and limit each nation's naval armaments. During the time Linton served on board *Iron Duke*, it was used mainly as a gunnery training vessel, although by the outbreak of the Second World War it had been moved to Scapa Flow, where it was used as a harbour defence ship.

Linton remained a Lieutenant until 1 July 1936, when the Admiralty announced that he had been promoted to the rank of Lieutenant Commander. He remained with *Iron Duke* until October 1938, at which time he was transferred to back to the Far East, where he was placed in command of the *Parthian*-class Royal Navy submarine HMS *Pandora*, commissioned in 1930. At the outbreak of the Second World War, *Pandora* was moved to the 8th Submarine Flotilla at Gibraltar to carry out patrol duties in the Mediterranean.

The *London Gazette* of Friday, 2 May 1941 carried an announcement from the Admiralty in Whitehall that while serving on board HMS *Pandora,* Lieutenant Commander John Wallace Linton had been awarded the Distinguished Service Cross, "for courage and determination in sinking two Italian supply ships".

After commanding HMS *Turbulent* since its launch over a year earlier, the *London Gazette* of Friday, 11 September 1942 included an article from the Admiralty, which in turn was dated Tuesday, 15 September 1942, describing Linton's next commendation.

> The King has been graciously pleased to give orders for the following Appointments to the Distinguished Service Order, and to approve the following Award:-
>
> For courage and skill in successful submarine patrols in H.M.S Turbulent:
>
> *To be a companion of the Distinguished Service Order:* Commander John Wallace Linton D.S.C., Royal Navy.

The qualifying criteria for the award of the DSO is for distinguished services during active operations against the enemy. Only one of the vessels sunk by *Turbulent* was a military one, and twenty of the torpedoes fired on six enemy vessels missed. Is this distinguished enough service to warrant such an award?

Under Linton's command, HMS *Turbulent* left its base at Algiers to begin its twelfth, and final, war patrol on 24 February 1943. It was never seen again.

Three months later, the *London Gazette* of Friday, 21 May 1943 carried an announcement from the Admiralty that Linton had been awarded the Victoria Cross for valour:

> From the outbreak of the War until H.M.S. *Turbulent*'s last patrol Commander Linton was constantly in command of submarines, and during that time inflicted great damage on the Enemy. He sank one Cruiser, one Destroyer, one U-boat, twenty-eight Supply Ships, some 100,000 tons in all, and destroyed three trains by gun-fire. In his last year he spent two hundred and fifty-four days at sea, submerged for

> nearly half the time, and his ship was hunted thirteen times and had two hundred and fifty depth charges aimed at her.
>
> His many and brilliant successes were due to his constant activity and skill, and the daring which never failed him when there was an enemy to be attacked.
>
> On one occasion, for instance, in H.M.S. *Turbulent*, he sighted a convoy of two Merchantmen and two Destroyers in mist and moonlight. He worked round ahead of the convoy and dived to attack it as it passed through the moon's rays. On bringing his sights to bear he found himself right ahead of a Destroyer. Yet he held his course till the Destroyer was almost on top of him, and when his sights came on the convoy he fired. His great courage and determination were rewarded. He sank one Merchantman and one Destroyer outright, and set the other Merchantman on fire so that she blew up.

In the same announcement, twenty-three other officers and men who had also served on HMS *Turbulent* received gallantry awards, "for bravery and devotion to duty in successful patrols".

It is interesting to note that although Linton's Victoria Cross was not officially listed as been a posthumous award, he received it two months after *Turbulent* went missing.

CHAPTER FOUR

The Attack on the *Nino Bixio*

The *Nino Bixio*, named after a nineteenth-century soldier and politician, was an Italian cargo vessel first launched on 19 October 1940 and owned by Gruppo Garibaldi, a shipping company from Genoa, Italy. It was operated on their behalf by one of its subsidiary companies, SA Co-operative di Navigazione.

On 16 August 1942, the *Nino Bixio* left the port of Benghazi in company with fellow Italian cargo vessel, the *Sestriere.* On board the two ships were several thousand Allied prisoners of war who had been captured during the North African campaign. Their destination was the city port of Brindisi in southern Italy, a distance of some 600 miles. The journey would not have been a pleasant one for those on board, even before the attack by HMS *Turbulent*, as average August temperatures in Benghazi generally saw daytime highs of 31°C (88°F).

Conditions in those temperatures would also have been poor, with an estimated 3,200 men sitting inside the darkened cargo hold of a steel-hulled vessel with no breeze or air conditioning to help reduce the heat and humidity. They also had little or no drinking water, and the only thing in place sanitation-wise were a limited number of oil drums.

The German army officer Captain H. Wilhelm compiled a report about the attack entitled, "Report on the torpedoing of the *Nino Bixio* on 17 August 1942, and the nine-day journey of the 1st Platoon on the Carley Float". The report in its entirety can be read on the website www.rommelsriposte.com and provides an excellent narrative about the convoy's journey leading up to the attack, as well as the aftermath.

It begins by describing how the convoy that *Nino Bixio* and *Sestriere* were part of left Benghazi at 1400 hours on 16 August. The Axis forces on board the *Nino Bixio* included the ship's Captain; a military commander (who was also a Captain), in overall charge; an Italian police Captain; a Lieutenant; forty Italian soldiers whose job it was to guard the prisoners; and finally, an Italian Lieutenant in charge of the ship's anti-aircraft contingent. The report also explained how many POWs were on each of the vessels.

The Italians had, for some unknown reason, gone to the unusual and rather time-consuming effort of determining which prisoners would be carried on each vessel depending on their surname. Those with surnames beginning with the letters A–L were placed on board the *Sestriere*, while those whose surnames began with the letters M–Z were placed on board the ill-fated *Nino Bixio*. Nearly all the prisoners were crammed into the ship's cargo holds which, for security reasons, were locked and greatly hindered the attempts to rescue the survivors.

The two Italian cargo vessels were escorted by two destroyers of the Italian navy, the *Saetta* and the *Nicoloso da Recco*, along with two Italian naval torpedo boats, the *Castore* and the *Orione*. The naval convoy had added aerial protection provided by the German Luftwaffe, which included three Junkers 88s and a Heinkel 111, along with two Italian Macchi C.200 aircraft.

According to the report, the first day of the journey had gone smoothly and was, by and large, uneventful. The beginning of the second day was exactly the same; the seas were calm, the skies were blue with not a cloud to be seen, and there were no Allied naval vessels or aircraft anywhere nearby. The route of the convoy took them past Crete and the Greek island of Cape Matapan, and by 1500 hours on 17 August, the western coastline of the Peloponnese would have been clearly in view.

Thirty minutes later, the *Sestriere*, which was sailing some 4 miles to the starboard of the *Nino Bixio*, clearly spotted something up ahead as it suddenly sounded its foghorn, not just in a single blast, but continuously, while at the same time turning hard to starboard. It is inconceivable that the Captain of the *Nino Bixio*, Antonio Raggio, did not hear the *Sestriere's* foghorn, despite the distance between the two ships, but for some inexcusable reason, he continued on the same course and took no defensive measures. Unbeknown to him, up ahead was the Royal Navy submarine, HMS *Turbulent*.

At just after 1530 hours, the British submarine, under the command of Commander John Linton, fired four torpedoes towards the two Italian cargo vessels, having absolutely no idea that the "cargo" the two vessels were carrying was, in fact, Allied prisoners of war. Immediately after firing its torpedoes, *Turbulent* dived to avoid being attacked itself by some of the convoy's escort vessels. One of the fired torpedoes had a gyroscope malfunction sending it so far off course it actually passed back above *Turbulent* on three occasions, fortunately missing it each time. The other three remaining torpedoes all struck the *Nino Bixio*, whilst the *Sestriere* escaped unscathed.

One of those that did strike did not detonate on impact, mainly because it did not hit the main body of the ship, but instead clipped the ship's rudder, albeit with sufficient force to disable it enough so that it was unable to steer in any direction other than round and round in uncontrollable circles.

Captain Wilhelm's report included the fact that the second torpedo fired by *Turbulent* struck the *Nino Bixio's* engine room, causing all the deck cargo to be blown overboard. It also caused a launch to be ripped from its holdings, which landed on the starboard gun placement killing one of the German guards, Sergeant Lukaschick, in the process.

The first two torpedoes fired struck the *Nino Bixio* on the starboard, causing it to list heavily in the same direction. Smoke escaped from the ruptured fog barrels, which made it difficult to see and gauge how low down in the water the vessel was.

The two remaining torpedoes both struck the main body of the *Nino Bixio.* One of them scored a direct hit on the ship's engine room, disabling the propulsion system and power supplies, which in turned caused it to explode. The other, meanwhile, sliced through the ship's hull, detonating the inside of No. 1 hold, which was where a large number of prisoners, most of them New Zealanders, had been placed before the ship set sail. In total 184 prisoners from No. 1 hold were killed. A number of French POWs in No. 2 hold and Indian POWs in No. 3 hold also perished in the attack.

In the immediate aftermath of the torpedoes striking the *Nino Bixio*, its deck, which was awash with blood, was not a sight for the feint hearted. Many of the men who had been stood there, mainly Italian guards, had been reduced to nothing more recognisable than human remains and body parts, such was the power of the explosion which forced itself up and out from within the bowels of the ship.

As might be expected in such circumstances, pandemonium was the order of the day, both amongst the surviving members of the crew as well as the POWs. The main aim for all those still alive, wounded or otherwise, was survival, saving wounded colleagues, and the thought of being rescued as quickly as possible.

Wilhelm's report explained that the guards, possibly because they believed the ship was going to sink, began to allow the POWs out of the cargo holds and up on to the deck, many of whom then proceeded to clamber up into the ship's superstructure, along with all the available launches and Carley floats. It would not be an exaggeration to describe it as a blind panic.

Despite the belief by many Allied POWs that the *Nino Bixio* would sink in the immediate aftermath of the attack, it remained afloat, but this did not prevent a number of them jumping overboard in anticipation of what might happen.

What hindered the operation to rescue those POWs still alive but trapped inside the ship's holds, was that in No. 1 hold, the lower level was separated from what is known as the shelter deck (a lightly constructed deck over the main deck of a ship covering a space that offers some protection from the weather without being completely enclosed) by two wooden ladders, both of which had been damaged and rendered unusable as a result of the attack.

The Italians did their best to try to save as many of the prisoners as they could, both from inside the holds of the stricken *Nino Bixio* and from the surrounding waters of the Mediterranean, where some survivors had taken refuge when they thought the ship was about to sink beneath the waves.

Part of Wilhelm's report described the chaos for some of those who had survived and jumped into the sea to escape what they believed was a sinking vessel. A large float was bobbing about in the water which had become so heavily occupied with German and Italian soldiers, along with a number of POWs, that it was struggling to stay above the surface of the water, and on more than one occasion the float capsized.

Besides the torpedo boats *Castore* and *Orione*, who were part of the convoy's escort, the Italians sent the destroyer *Luigi Cadorna* to help with the rescue operation as well as a hospital ship, the *Cordona*, to treat those who had been wounded in the attack.

For those who had jumped into the water, some drowned immediately, while others reached makeshift rafts and drifted around the Mediterranean for a number of days without food or water. Those on board who had survived the carnage were hauled up on deck by rope. The injured were treated by medical officers. Despite extensive damage, the *Nino Bixio* did not sink. The ship was towed by an escorting destroyer to Navarino in southern Greece, where the dead were buried. The surviving POWs were transferred ashore and those fit enough were shipped, after a short stay in Corinth, to Bari, Italy, to a prisoner of war camp where they spent the rest of the war.

Eyewitness accounts from POWs on board the *Nino Bixio* also provide an excellent illustration of what happened in the immediate aftermath of the attack. The following is an account from Sapper Bill Rudd of the 2nd/7th Field Company, Royal Australian Engineers. Bill survived the attack and passed away on 29 October 2019, just shy of his 101st birthday. His account appears here with the kind permission of his son, Tony.

> All I can remember after embarkation into the forward hold was finding, on the steel mezzanine deck that ran around the hold, a space between a

South African sergeant and a Kiwi private. It was incredibly hot and stuffy and the rhythmic beat of the engines and the slow roll of the ship made dozing almost a permanent state of mind and the time of night or day of little consequence.

I remember a sudden tremendous thud and the "whoompf" of the torpedo bursting into the hold. The ship slowed immediately and I learned later that another torpedo had struck the engine room amidships. Looking down on the bottom of the hold was like watching a surreal merry-go-round. It was still daylight and the clear white and jade-green water was swirling around in a clockwise direction with bodies, clothing, petrol drums that had served as urinals and all sorts of gear revolving at a mad pace.

The water was also rising rapidly and the smell of cordite hung thickly in the foetid air. Men were pressing towards the ladder leading upwards to the deck and the human tide carried me with it. Somehow it carried me also to the deck and the sight of the open sky and the fresh smell of the sea was unbelievably welcome.

On deck it was a scene of complete confusion. Those on the deck immediately above the hold, mainly guards, had been blown to bits. There were remains of humans hanging in the rigging and body parts littered the bloody deck. An anti-aircraft gun there was a mangled twisted piece of steel, crushed under steel deck beams which had been hurled upwards by the force of the explosion and then crashed back onto the ship. POWs were pouring up from other holds and many, mainly Indians, were jumping off the decks into the sea. The red-bearded Captain of the ship, with a revolver in his hand, was shouting orders and trying to restore some semblance of sanity and discipline among his crew.

The *Nino Bixio* was settling lower into the water but did not appear to be sinking and ropes appeared from somewhere and those that had reached the open deck were hauling badly injured mates and bodies out of the watery hell of Number 1 hold.

One of the escorting Italian destroyers that had been circling the *Nino Bixio* dropping depth charges through the carpet of bobbing heads of those that had leapt overboard, broke off to attach a cable to her as daylight began to fade and began the slow haul toward the land that could be seen to starboard.

It was a long night, but by daylight the *Nino Bixio* had been beached off Novarino Harbour in Greece and rescue teams of both Germans and Italians came aboard to supervise the evacuation of the ship. Unwounded New Zealanders and Australians were left to the last and were put to work cleaning up the ship, reeking with the smell of death. Finally, they too were ferried ashore.

I was dropped off with some other Australians from a lorry that pulled up at some sort of a warehouse. It had three tiers of "shelves" and I think was probably some short of drying shed for fruit. This was plentiful as it was autumn and we had been able to get some figs and tomatoes thrown at us by friendly Greeks who risked retribution by trying to get anywhere near us. I found a berth with three French Foreign Legionnaires caught at Bir Hakim. We got on well. Late that night, I was called out to have all my body hair shaved off. I was given some sort of naval clothing and loaded into a lorry for Patras. I never saw my French mates again. Eventually I was loaded into another Italian ship - not a hospital one. As it happened, once again I had been allotted to the forward hold and once again I was awakened from a drowse by a sudden thunderous noise. But this time it was the release of the ship's anchor chain from its storage compartment. We had arrived in Bari Harbour - "bella Italia" at last!

We were marched through the streets to a railway station amid a hostile reception by the citizens of Bari, loaded into railway wagons and taken on a long a slow journey north. I have no remembrance of time, but eventually we were taken off in darkness and marched to what I later found out to be Campo di concentramento No 57 Gruppignano. By then I really didn't care where I was. I was lousy, weak with dysentery and had contracted jaundice. Fortunately, I was able to respond to a voice yelling out in the dark, "Anybody there from Melbourne?" That voice belonged to Cpl Gordon Dare of the 2/24th Infantry Battalion. He had been captured in Derna in April 1941, and was already a hardened "kriegie".

> He took me under his wing despite my allocation to a different hut in a different compound. He nursed me back to health through that terrible winter and I was later to be best man at his wedding back in Melbourne.

Bill's description of the attack is not only told in so much detail, but without stating the obvious, it tells the story from the other side, the victim's side. Such a tale is very rarely told, mainly because there are not usually that many survivors who have lived to tell it.

His words change what would otherwise have been just a total number of those who died into detailed information about the trauma, fear, pain and suffering the men went through in such circumstances. It makes it so much more personal, real and impactive. It changes from being a simple written account into a clear and precise picture of the events as they unfolded.

The story of the attack on the *Nino Bixio* by HMS *Turbulent*, when seen through Bill's eyes, takes on an entire new meaning because it does not stop with the attack. It continues on with the next three years of his life in captivity, and his return home to his friends, family and civilian life, experiences that those men on board the *Nino Bixio* who were killed in the attack, or in the immediate aftermath, would never know.

The POW camp Bill found himself incarcerated in was Campo PG 57, which was situated in northern Italy, some 80 kilometres north-east of Trieste, would be his new home for the next three years.

> The numbering of Italian prison camps commenced in early 1942, and by that time, the prison buildings consisted of two self-contained compounds, each

with its own cook-house, ablution block, recreation huts and Orderly Rooms. The dormitory huts were made of double wooden walls located on concrete foundations, with a metaled roof, and one single heating stove, for which there never appeared to be any fuel.

Sleeping accommodation was in wooden double decker bunks in groups of eight. Each hut held approximately fifty prisoners, and the Hut Commander slept in an area which doubled as a "Hut Office". Each compound contained some twenty huts, so that there would be approximately 1,000 POWs in each compound.

From the Camp looking north through the perimeter barbed wire system, there was a spectacular view of the Dolomites and the mountains of nearby Yugoslavia. The scenery was magnificent, even when viewed through barbed wire spectacles.

The Camp was controlled by Lieutenant Colonel V.E. Calcaterra, formerly of the elite Carabinieri Police. Calcaterra, who prided himself on his strict discipline, and who boasted that his prison was "escape-proof", was justifiably "Enemy Number One" to every ANZAC POW in the camp. He was succinctly summed up by AVW "Bluey" Rymer, a British wireless operator/air gunner, as "a short-arsed, fat-gutted little shit". If you were sitting on one side of the camp and you did not get up and stand to attention, it was into the boob, bread and water.

> Initially PG Campo 57 was home to men from a number of different countries, including Australia, Britain, Cyprus, Greece, New Zealand and Yugoslavia, but once the Italians reorganised the numbering of their POW camp system it became the main Italian camp for Australian and New Zealand "other ranks" only. The officers were then separated according to their nationality, with Australians being held at PG Campo 78, at Sulmona, and New Zealanders at Campo 52, at Chiavari.
>
> By June 1942, PG 57 held some 2,000 Australian and New Zealand POWs. As the fierce fighting around El Alamein saw many Allied POWs taken by Rommel's forces, who were then handed over to the Italians, the Italian authorities pushed forward their expansion plans, and two new compounds, 3 and 4, arose to extend the already operative compounds 1 and 2. By the end of 1942, the four compounds were home to some 4,000 ANZAC POW, a figure not much less than the total number of AIF POW in all German camps.

It is strange to think that the experience Bill Rudd describes only took place because of the actions of HMS *Turbulent.* When asked when his father first found out that it was HMS *Turbulent* who had carried out the attack on the *Nino Bixio*, and what his subsequent feelings towards the British were, Bill's son Tony Rudd replied as follows:

> Dad never said when he was aware they had been torpedoed by the British. I have a feeling, though, that they knew the rules of war, sink enemy shipping,

> regardless of cargo, human or otherwise. Collateral damage. They would have known the only attack would come from allied air or sea forces. They had great respect for Rommel and also knew that the only way Rommel would be defeated was by starving him of supply. I guess they put two and two together.
>
> He explained more of the circumstances to me later, but he was never bitter about it being the British. At least he never told me.
>
> He had great admiration for the ship's captain, Antonio Raggio, and the way he compassionately handled the hell he had been handed.

Another survivor of the attack on the *Nino Bixio* was Private Charles Watkins, a New Zealander with the 25th Battalion, New Zealand Infantry. By July 1942, with his basic training behind him, he was involved in the fighting during the North African campaign, where he was captured and became a prisoner of war. After having initially been held at a detention camp near Benghazi, along with more than 3,000 other Allied POWs, he was placed on board the *Nino Bixio*. Fortunately for Charles, he was far enough away and high enough up from the entry points of the torpedoes in No.1 hold and the engine room to have survived.

What follows is his personal account of *Turbulent's* attack in August 1942.

> I was playing bridge with another Kiwi and two Australians. I'd taken six tricks, but I couldn't see

how I was going to take the others. The torpedo then burst into the hold, ending the game.

It was no laughing matter I can tell you. There was a lot of swearing and yelling and jumping around. We were in humid semi-darkness. The explosion had wrecked the two wooden ladders to the bottom half of the hold now submerged in the surging sea. When the rescue started, we pulled up some of the injured with ropes and others on a bit of a stretcher made from the remains of one of the wooden ladders. But it was a hopeless task. Nothing could be done for those screaming for help in the water. You had to walk over dead bodies to move anywhere.

The two ladders leading from the catwalk to the deck were still intact and slowly those in the upper part of the hold managed to get to the deck. Some jumped overboard, but it was now obvious that the bulkhead had held and the *Nino Bixio* was not going to sink.

Medical facilities were minimal, but some sort of order began to emerge, although it was too late to save many of the wounded.

The *Sestriere* had sailed out of sight and one of the escort boats was busy running a towline to the *Nino Bixio*. Somehow the night passed and next morning we found ourselves beached and help was arriving from land.

> The process of unloading the wounded began, but most of the casualties had gone into the sea. We were among the last to be taken off the ship.

Charles Watkins was initially sent to Camp PG 107, before being moved to one of the smaller work camps at Torre di Confine. At some time during his captivity he managed to escape, but was soon recaptured. However, instead of being returned to his camp at Torre di Confine, he was sent to Stalag IV-G, a German POW camp for NCOs and enlisted men in Oschatz, a small town situated between Leipzig and Dresden.

As of 16 March 1945, the camp held a total of 5,233 Allied POWs, who were assigned to a total of 76 separate work camps. Charles and his comrades were liberated on 24 April 1945, which in New Zealand was 25 April; ANZAC day, an important memorial day for New Zealanders and Australians, and a coincidence that was very much to Charles' liking.

On 6 November 1948, Charles married Mary Richardson, with whom he had six children. He passed away on 26 June 2013, when he was 93 years of age.

Gordon Watkins, Charles' son, was also asked when his father had found out the *Nino Bixio* had been attacked by a British submarine, and what his feelings were. This was his reply:

> I don't remember when dad found out that the *Nino Bixio* had been attacked by the *Turbulent*, but I know that he was not happy about it. I remember that he believed Prime Minister Winston Churchill was aware of the attack before it happened and did not take measures to stop it even though he knew that there were many allied servicemen on

> board. I remember seeing on social media, or on a NZ news website, a photograph of dad holding a document that he believed confirmed Churchill's knowledge of the imminent attack. He also said that he believed the attack wasn't stopped because the Allied leadership did not want to let the enemy know Bletchley Park had cracked German communication codes.

Among the other survivors of the attack were three brothers, Gerald, Malcolm and Peter Norton-Knight, who had enlisted into the newly formed 3rd Australian Anti-Tank Artillery Regiment on 9 July 1940 at Paddington, New South Wales, as part of the all-volunteer 2nd Australian Imperial Force, which in turn was assigned to the Australian 8th Infantry Division raised for overseas service.

After just two months of training, the regiment had left Australia in November 1940 and made its way to the Middle East, arriving there a few weeks later. It then underwent further training, before moving on to Amiriya in Egypt in early March 1941. It was not long after this that the regiment saw its first action, and from then on there was little in the way of respite for the Australian soldiers, who fought at Tobruk, Tripoli and during the First Battle of El Alamein in the Western Desert.

The three Norton-Knight brothers had been captured by German forces on 27 July 1942, the last day of the of the fighting at El Alamein, and on Sunday, 16 August all three were on board the *Nino Bixio* when it was attacked by HMS *Turbulent*.

With both of his brothers injured in the attack, Lance Sergeant Gerald Norton-Knight remained on board to assist with removing the dead and wounded from inside the vessel.

Once the badly damaged *Nino Bixio* had reached Brindisi, to where it had been towed, Gerald was transferred to the Italian POW camp PG 29 near Veano, in northern Italy. He also spent time at Campo PG 75 in Bari, and Campo PG 82 at Laterini, before ending up at Campo PG 57, Grupignano, where he met up with his brother, Malcolm.

On 8 September 1943, the Italians capitulated and surrendered to the Allies, leading to a mass break out from Campo 57. One of those who took part in the escape was Gerald Norton-Knight, but just five days later he was captured by German forces and sent to Stalag 18A at Wolfsburg in Austria, where it is believed he remained until the end of the war.

Having initially survived the attack on the *Nino-Bixio*, Gerald's brother, Gunner Peter Norton-Knight subsequently died of diphtheria on 25 August 1942 at the 8th Evacuation Hospital at Caserta, approximately 15 miles north of Naples. He was 31 years of age.

The final Norton-Knight brother to survive, Gunner Malcolm Osborne Norton-Knight, was also wounded during the attack. He was transferred to an Italian military hospital to have his wounds treated, and it was probably the 8th Evacuation Hospital at Caserta, the same one his brother, Peter, was sent to.

It is more than likely that Malcolm took part in the same mass escape from Campo PG 57 as his brother Gerald on 8 September 1943. After he was recaptured, he was sent to Stalag VIII-B POW camp, located close to the village of Lamsdorf, in Silesia. Malcolm made it home after the war and died in New South Wales on 15 May 1980, when he was 63 years of age.

While tales of survival are always good to hear, the obvious question to ask, however, is why did the attack happen in the first place? Why did HMS *Turbulent* attack the *Nino Bixio*?

The natural and obvious assumption to make is because Commander Linton had absolutely no idea that the Italian cargo vessel was carrying Allied POWs, and had received no intelligence reports to suggest otherwise.

The chilling alternative is that the British authorities were fully aware of the "cargo" the *Nino Bixio* was carrying below its decks, and decided that sinking it was more important than the lives of the men on board.

Such a scenario did have precedent. On 9 December 1941, the Italian merchant vessel the *Sebastiano Veniero*, which had been commandeered by German forces, was attacked by the British *Grampus*-class, minelaying submarine, HMS *Porpoise*, off the Peloponnese coast in southern Greece. Its "cargo" at the time was an estimated 2,000 mainly South African, New Zealand and British Allied POWs captured during the fighting of the North African campaign. Around 450 of these men died in the attack.

What is interesting is that the day before, the Naval Section of British Military Intelligence sent a document entitled 'Naval Headlines 159' to Prime Minister Winston Churchill, which included information concerning Italian military matters obtained from intercepting radio messages. One read as follows: 'The motor-ship "Veniero" will leave Benghazi for Italy at 4pm/8, with 2,000 prisoners of war on board.' Clear proof that the *Veniero* was carrying Allied prisoners of war. The attack did not take place until 1435 hours the following day, meaning Churchill, the British government and the hierarchy of the Royal Navy knew more than 24 hours before the *Veniero* was attacked that it was carrying Allied POWs. This provided plenty of time for the information to have been forwarded to the submarine flotillas operating throughout the Mediterranean Sea.

It is clear that no such message was received by the commanders of patrolling Royal Navy submarines in the Mediterranean, as it is difficult to comprehend that they would have carried out an attack on any enemy vessel they knew for certain was carrying British and Allied POWs. Why this vital piece of information was not passed on can only be guessed at. Possibly the British authorities did not want to risk the Italians working out that their radio messages were being intercepted. But what is the point of possessing information that could save British and Allied lives if it is not then acted upon?

Sadly, there are several examples of Allied vessels attacking Axis ships carrying POWs, although whether they knew what they were carrying at the time cannot be verified. On 14 February 1942, just two months after the attack on the *Sebastiano Veniero*, a similar tragedy struck the 4,000-ton Italian merchant ship the *Ariosto*, when it was attacked and sunk off the coast of Cape Afrika, Tunisia, by the Royal Navy submarine, HMS *P.38*. The *Ariosto*, with a crew of 116, had been transporting 294 Allied POWs from Tunisia across the Mediterranean to Italy, where they were to be transferred to POW camps.

Of the Allied POWs on board, 138 were killed along with 26 Italian crewmen of the *Ariosto.* As for HMS *P.38*, it had only been commissioned on 17 October 1941, and whilst preparing to attack an Italian supply convoy in the waters off Tripoli on 23 February 1942, just eight days after sinking the *Ariosto*, it was located and sunk by depth charges dropped from the Italian torpedo boat, *Circe.* There were no survivors from a crew of thirty-two.

HM Submarine *Upholder*, under the command of Lieutenant Commander Malcolm David Wanklyn VC DSO & Two Bars, attacked and sank the Italian merchant vessel

SS *Tembien* about 25 miles west of Tripoli on the evening of 27 February 1942.At the time, the *Tembien* was en route to the Italian mainland carrying 468 Allied POWs, all captured during the fighting in North Africa. At just after 1900, the *Tembien* was struck by two torpedoes fired by HMS *Upholder.* The attack resulted in the deaths of 390 POWs, 68 Italian crew members and 10 German guards.

At around 1730 hours on 13 October 1942, the Royal Navy U-class submarine HMS *Unruffled* attacked and sank the 1,000-ton Italian cargo ship *Loreto*, 4 miles off Cape Gallo, just north of Sicily. Having been struck by two torpedoes, the stricken vessel sank within fifteen minutes. Of the approximately 400 Allied POWs it was carrying, many of whom were Indian soldiers, 129 were killed, along with 18 members of a crew of 57.

The last of these tragic events took place on 14 November 1942, when the Royal Navy S-class submarine, HMS *Sahib*, attacked and sank the British built, 1,500-ton Italian registered transport vessel, *Scillin.*

The *Scillin* had left Tripoli on 13 November, en route to Sicily, with 814 Allied POWs crammed into her hold. This resulted in massive over- crowding, with the added elements of extreme heat and poor sanitary conditions. The *Scillin* was approximately 10 miles north of Capo Milazzo, Sicily, and nearing the end of its journey when tragedy struck.

HMS *Sahib*, based in Malta, was on its second war patrol and cruising on the surface when it came across the *Scillin.* *Sahib* opened fire from its deck gun before deploying a single torpedo, which struck the *Scillin* in its forward hold, the subsequent explosion causing it to sink.

Only 27 of the 814 Allied POWs on board survived the attack, along with 35 members of the *Scillin's* crew, which included the Captain. All the men were rescued by *Sahib*, who stayed on the surface to pick them up, despite the potential danger this placed her in from attack by Italian naval vessels that were in the area at the time.

Imagine the feelings of sickness, shock and horror of *Sahib's* Commander, Lieutenant John Bromage and his crew when they heard the English accents of twenty-seven of the survivors they plucked from the sea. Realisation would have quickly set in that not only had they attacked and sunk a vessel that was carrying British prisoners of war, but they had also killed an unknown number of their comrades in arms.

Despite the British authorities being aware that the *Scillin* was carrying a large number of Allied POWs following an intercepted coded message, the attempts to protect the source of this intelligence went as far as holding an inquiry into the sinking, where Lieutenant Bromage had to defend his actions. Thankfully for him, and the preservation of common decency, he was cleared of any wrong doing. The fact that an inquiry ever took place was incredulous as the *Sahib* had been directed to the area where they intercepted and sank the *Scillin* by the Royal Navy's Mediterranean Fleet Command, based in Malta, who had more than likely been in possession of the intelligence that the *Scillin* was carrying British and Allied POWs.

Another tactic deployed by the British in their attempts to protect intelligence obtained from their Ultra intercepts was to have RAF aircraft fly aerial reconnaissance in the skies above the intended targets and report such sightings to the submarines below, who would then carry out the attacks. Those on board the enemy vessels would then naturally assume that any attack had been carried out because they had been identified by RAF aircraft.

The decision was taken by the British government that the details concerning the sinking of the *Scillin* and the loss of so many Allied POWs should be kept secret. This was so as not to alarm members of the public and possibly affect public morale back home, which was an important factor in the nation's war effort. This meant that the families of those who had been on board when it was sunk did not find out the truth about how their loved ones died until 1996. In the fifty-four years between those two events, many of the relatives themselves had died, meaning that they went to their own graves without ever having been told the truth.

CHAPTER FIVE

Letters from John Deller – Crew member of HMS *Turbulent*

John Deller was a member of HM Submarine *Turbulent*'s crew, who died when the vessel was lost in March 1943. He had enlisted in the Royal Navy when he was 23 years of age, on 31 March 1941, and transferred to submarines just two months later.

He had a brother, Jim Deller, in New Zealand, who wrote a number of letters to him during the war, and it was Jim's son, also John Deller, who kindly agreed for the letters to appear here.

Only when reading through the letters did it become clear that John Deller had, in fact, been one of *Turbulent*'s original crew members, serving aboard even before its sea trials were conducted. This means that the letters not only provide a direct insight into the life of a trainee submariner and life on board a wartime submarine, but are also important historical documents in their own right. How many other similar letters have survived is unknown, but if they are the only ones to have survived, which is quite possible, then they could be regarded as priceless.

The first of the letters is dated 13 November 1940, when Able Seaman John Deller was 21 years of age and stationed at HMS St Vincent, a shore establishment at Gosport, Hampshire. Prior to the outbreak of the Second World War, the base had been used as a training facility for boys and juniors, but with the war under way it became multi-functional. Its main purpose became the training of Fleet Air Arm officers and torpedo units, as well as being used as a signals school barracks.

> Dear Jim and Lynne,
>
> No doubt you will have been wondering how the world is treating me, well, life in the R.N. isn't so dusty, in fact I'm in the best of health and spirit. How are you going along? You've certainly got the laugh over us, no black out or restrictions, etc. I suppose when this letter reaches you, you will be enjoying the summer weather.
>
> Will you have the turkey and "pud" on the beach? Or will it be a bit too draughty?
>
> […]
>
> There's one good thing about the navy, and that is that you get around. On the way to Iceland, we stopped a couple of days in Glasgow. The people up there are very generous and really decent all round, we had a good time up there anyway.
>
> We had to work our passage on the ship, mostly "look out" duties, you should have seen me on the

> bridge during the "middle watch". Boy, was it breezy! We did half an hour on 1 hour off, so you can bet I took a trip or two down to the galley for a nice cup of coffee.
>
> Lord Gort [Commander-in-Chief of the British Expeditionary Force (BEF), whose reputation had been done no harm by the successful evacuation of British and Allied forces from the beaches of Dunkirk] accompanied us on the outward voyage, we were frequently seen together on the bridge, only I was working. I'll bet he felt slightly lowered in my presence, eh!
>
> We only stayed on the island a week, quite long enough, however, it's a miserable dump. The inhabitants wouldn't speak to us. They regarded us as invaders. I quite understand that, but they'd be a lot worse off if Jerry had occupied the place.

The journey to Iceland would have been from the docks at Greenock, out across the cold and uninviting waters of the North Sea, before arriving in Reykjavik, and would have no doubt included at least one escorting vessel. On their arrival, John Deller and his colleagues would have found themselves staying at HMS *Balder II,* a camp at Hvitanes, near to the city's football stadium, which would have been very basic with the living accommodation being nothing more inviting than Nissan huts. There was also HMS *Balder I*, which was to be found at the port of Reykjavik, believed to have been a *Sleipner*-class destroyer.

John Deller's letter continued:

The force to which we were attached had been there for five months, we returned with them and were not to be excluded from the 10 days leave that had been granted them.

I stayed for a week with a Mess-mate, Jack, with his family in Cumberland, a grand little spot up in the Lake District. It was hard to realise a war was in progress.

I took Jack's sister out most of the week. Jack is courting so we made up a foursome, there are plenty of dances up there, rather countryfied, but very sociable. I think we went to four, one started at 10pm and ended at 3am, rather a nocturnal affair, don't you think? I also went for a swim and a few walks in the country, it was a real tonic for me, more like a holiday. You can guess I was sorry to leave, but I may make another trip up there in the future.

I spent the remaining three days at home, what a difference. I was naturally pleased to be home for a few days, but it was dead. The longest raid ever had to take place while I was there, 6.30pm until 8.30am., 14 hours, what a game, eh!

I returned to my depot, Chatham on the Thurs. another miserable hole, but my stay there however was cut short for at 10.30am. Sat. I volunteered for a torpedo course. I left at 12am the same day, and was at Gosport by 8pm, a quick move and a good one. The barracks here are pretty decent, airy, nice beds and good grub.

This torpedo course is rather complicated, consisting mainly in electricity, something entirely new to me, but I find it quite interesting, and I think I shall make it ok. I expect I shall be here for about six weeks, might finish in time for Xmas leave.

Well, I'll take this opportunity of wishing you both a happy Christmas. I expect you'll be hearing from me before then though.

Well, cheers and all the best.

Yours Aff.
John

P.S. Have you got Jimmy under your thumb yet Lynne? He's easy, I know from experience.

This letter was dated 30 August 1941, when Able Seaman John Deller was serving aboard HMS *Oberon*, an *Odin*-class submarine first commissioned in August 1927. After ten years of service it had been placed in reserve in 1937, before being re-commissioned as a Royal Naval vessel on 2 August 1939. The submarine remained in service until it was decommissioned for a second and final time on 5 July 1944.

HMS *Oberon* was built at Chatham dockyards and was one of twenty O-class submarines that were built with long range patrol capabilities in mind and had come about as a direct result of Japan's refusal to renew the Anglo-Japanese Alliance in 1922. This in turn caused uneasiness at the Admiralty to such a degree that the O-class design came in to being. The submarines were not without their problems, one being that to accommodate the need for them to potentially be able to travel long distances, they had additional external fuel tanks which were prone to leaking. It has also been reported that they were not the easiest of vessels to operate and manoeuvre below the surface.

At 270 feet in length, 28 feet in width, and with 8 torpedo tubes, it was noticeably larger than the previous class of submarines, but this came at a price in the shape of a 2-knot reduction in speed.

Because of the number of times *Oberon* had found itself back in port under-going repairs and maintenance work, its crew had lovingly nick-named it HMS *Oh Be Joyful*, as on each occasion this happened the crew received additional periods of shore leave.

Oberon was also the first Royal Naval vessel to take an ASDIC set to sea for operational purposes. There is debate as to what the acronym actually stood for, but one suggestion is Anti-Submarine Detection Investigation Committee, named after the group that progressed and approved its use. The Americans also had it, but they called it SONAR, which stands for Sound Navigation Ranging.

In essence this was an instrument which sent out an acoustic pulse through the water and then measured the distance of an object struck by the sound wave by timing how long the pulse of the echo took to return to the receiver. This provided the operator with an accurate range of how far away the submarine was. The ASDIC's transmitter was located on the underneath of the ship or submarine, but if the vessel it was attached to was travelling in excess of 18 knots, or in choppy seas, contacts of enemy vessels was harder to pinpoint accurately.

It was used extensively by the British and American navies throughout the war to locate and track enemy submarines. The tell-tale sign if a target had been located was an extended noise, like a beep or a ping. The actual process of trying to locate enemy submarines was a constant one, which gave the Allied vessel the added advantage of feeling somewhat secure in the knowledge that they were highly unlikely to be caught unawares by the actions of alien submarines.

Watching the ASDIC screens for warning of enemy vessels was a skill that not everybody could master in order to correctly translate images they saw on the screen. In a comparatively short period of time, John Deller had become a relatively experienced ASDIC operative aboard HMS *Oberon*. A well-trained operative could determine the distance between the vessels, what direction they were travelling in and even how fast they were travelling. This was an aspect of the operator's role that was extremely important, as there were more than just submarines that sailed beneath the waves. The last thing a commander of a submarine wanted was to be going on a wild goose chase, only to find out that he was in fact up against a whale, an underwater rock face, or a large school of fish, rather than an enemy submarine. An experienced and reliable ASDIC operator was an invaluable crew member, and one that any commander would want to have on board his vessel.

Submarine crews had a precarious enough existence as it was, but a good commander knew what it took to keep himself and his crew alive. They knew that inclement weather and being brave enough to dive deep were both aids to their survival, and could help prevent them from being identified by an enemy hunting them down. Travelling on silent running and at a slow speed could literarily be a life saver, as the faster a submarine travelled at, the more noise its propellers made, thus making it easier to locate and identify.

Being located by an enemy was as good as a death sentence. If the hunter was another submarine the end was likely to come via a torpedo. If it was a surface vessel, then the weapon of choice was depth charges. Either version wasn't a positive conclusion for the crew of the submarine in question. The trouble for a surface vessel was it had to try to guess what setting to place its depth charges on, so that when they exploded they were as close to the submarine as possible. The only way of effectively doing this was to take into account the depth of the submarine at the last known contact.

The best thing that a hunted submarine could do was to put as much distance as possible between itself and its attacker, as a clear contact would usually be lost after a distance of 300 yards. In some cases this meant a submarine diving to extremely low depths. Six hundred feet was not unheard of in such circumstances.

Quite often the fight was not between two commanders, but between the commander of the hunted submarine and the ASDIC operator of the attacking vessel. Some of the sudden movements that submarine commanders made whilst trying to escape their attackers would be very acute, making life for their crews extremely uncomfortable, but this was a small price to pay if it ultimately saved the submarine and the lives of those on board. It was usually very small margins that decided the outcomes of these contests, and whether men lived or died.

As well as including John Deller among its former crew, *Oberon* was also the first submarine that John Linton, the future commander of HMS *Turbulent*, had served on when it was part of the 5th Submarine Flotilla.

For most of 1941 *Oberon* had largely been involved in training exercises, many of which had been for the Commanding Officers Qualifying course, although between 22 March and 13 April, the submarine had completed her fourth war patrol in the Bay of Biscay, off the west coast of France.

By the time John Deller had written the following letter he had been on submarines for just three months. On the day it was dated, 30 August 1941, the crew were on a break from their training exercise duties in the River Clyde.

> Dear Jim and Lynne,
>
> Your welcome letter received last week. It sure was a treat to hear from you. Thanks a lot for the PO, but really, you shouldn't have done it. Incidentally, as far as finance goes I am not doing too bad. My daily rate of pay is now 6/9 per day and together with duty free cigs and one or two other little privileges, am quite well loaded. As a note of interest "Churchman's" are now my favourite. Who would smoke "Woodbines" when the best are available at the price of 20 for 7 shillings?
>
> I shall probably be going home for a few days leave in a month's time, so will duly lash pop and the boys up with the necessary.
>
> This leave by the way, if it materialises, will be the first for five months, so I reckon I've earnt it.
>
> I doubt if the old burgh has changed at all, as you know London and the surrounding districts have not been visited by Jerry of late, not to any great extent anyway.

Have been on this boat now four months, so know more or less my way around, although never a day passes but something crops up about which I was previously uninformed. There must be thousands of valves on the boat and as yet I only know a quarter of them, not that they are directly concerned with me, but it is just a matter of interest to know them.

Can you picture old Fich at the "Helm"? I haven't been told, but I bet the old forehead wrinkles a little while concentrating on the course.

I wish it were possible to show you around this tub, I'm sure you'd be amazed. I could spin a yarn or two about some of our little experiences, maybe that will be possible one of these days, eh!

[...]

Have almost got another home here. We always stay at the same house when ashore and the "old girl" treats me like one of the family, she gave me five pairs of hand knitted socks the other week, also a real toff.

Four of us went for a coach trip last Sat. to a small coastal village, it was so out of the way, it did not even boast a pub. It was a marvellous day and we could not resist the temptation of having a swim, not having the necessary equipment we had to resort to old fashioned paddling style, probably made it all the more enjoyable, but oh boy! was it good.

Jim, I resent the crack about my writing, at the moment we are charging our battery and the vibration from our diesels is terrific, does that excuse me this time. I always could find an excuse, couldn't I? I'm not writing it on the deck anyway.

Well, here's hoping you all keep in the pink as well as I do.

You won't do far wrong then, 11st 10lb now, and no corporation.

Cheers, and all the very best.

Yours aff.
John.

The next letter John Deller sent was dated 8 October 1941. This date was significant as it was just two days before he officially began serving on board HMS *Turbulent.*

Dear Jim and Lynne,

Was very pleased to hear from you again, and pleased to learn that you are all fit and well.

I returned here today after the days leave at home, the first for six months, so consider I earnt it, eh! What do you think? Dad had a week off so we kept one another company on several occasions.

Pete happened to be home at the same time, so one morning Pete, Dad and I visited Epping in the car and logged Frank round to the nearest local, needless to say we carried out the ceremony of wetting your babies [sic] "brainbox", if I hadn't intervened they would have drowned the poor little "mite".

Have now left the "Oberon" for good, and am waiting to pick up a brand new S/M, she's a honey, I can see a lot will be expected from us. "Turbulent" is the name so watch out for it.

Until such time as she is ready we are just loafing around reporting at 0915 each morning and returning each day at 1500 for dinner when we have finished for the day. Nice work, eh! However it is only compensation in advance so to speak, for you can take it from me, it's far from honey at times.

[...]

If and when the occasion arrives re your liability for conscription, "what do you propose doing", Jim? If my advice is of any consequence, take my tip and have another go in the M.N. failing that, the R.N. you are a pretty adaptable bloke so you'd be ok whatever you go in.

The situation sure does change a deal. I am pleased to see that this country has at last recognised Russia's morals, it took a war to prove it though.

If ever a country has had to swallow its own words, this one has.

Well, I will say cheerio for now. Once again thanking you for your letter, hoping that you are all keeping ok.

So with love to you all

Yours affect.
John.

When John Deller sends his next letter, *Turbulent* is still in the Vickers Armstrong yard at Barrow where it was being built. His address on the letter is shown as simply, "Barrow", and is dated 11 November 1941.

Dear James and Lynne,

Received your welcome letter whilst at home during the weekend, I also had the pleasure of reading your letter, Lynne, to Dad, pleased to know you are still enjoying life in spite of mumps, abscesses and baby's ailments, still all these little troubles are sent to try us, and judging by the tone of your letters, you do not seem unduly worried, that's the stuff and keep it up.

I was rather surprised on learning that you weighed only 10 stone 12 lbs, as we were only talking about that tight fitting suit you used to wear, you remember, the double breasted. I guess it fits you ok now, don't disappoint me by saying that you have dispensed with it. I shouldn't worry about weight though. I gained two stone during my time in the R.N. but am pleased to say that I have lost one of them. Turning the scale now at 10 stone 10 lbs and I'll warrant I'd lose another stone within a month of pre-war routine, and I can say with all sincerity that I was a fitter man then than I am now.

[...]

Have just heard the nine o'clock news, 10 ships and 3 Destroyers sunk in the Med and the old subs have been doing their stuff too.

My holidays, as I call them, will soon be over, for the boat is fast approaching completion. I guess we shall have a sticky task to perform, but don't worry, I'll be fine if our luck holds good.

You asked me to tell you more about S/Ms, well, that's hardly possible these days, without infringing the censor's regulations, and I would hate to do that. I can say however, that half the machinery pipes and other gadgets are not to be found on surface craft. So we have quite an individual experience. They are propelled by two methods, diesels and electric motors, the latter obtaining its power from the batteries which are charged by the diesels whilst cruising on the surface at night, this I expect is more or less common knowledge, but sorry, I cannot divulge more.

If ever you get the chance though, you certainly ought to look over one, if only to have some idea of what it's like for me on the Turbulent.

The best part of the sub service is the relaxation of discipline and the extra pay which in my case is now 8/-.

Will probably write to you again when we have completed our trials.

That'll do for the present. Wishing you all the very best of luck.

Yours affectionately
John.

The next letter is dated 24 November 1941, just nine days before *Turbulent* was commissioned into the Royal Navy.

Dear All,

Received your welcome letter this morning, also the cigs Dad, for which I thank you very much.

Sorry to hear that Ralph is very queer, he doesn't seem to have too much luck, does he? Still, I guess your visit bucked him up a little.

I've had a real soft job lately, while the lads have been provisioning and ammunitioning the boat, I've been sitting in the office answering the telephone, doing a bit of writing and general administration. Can you imagine me taking to office work? It's alright for a change, but as a regular job, well it wouldn't suit me at all. Incidentally, no comment was made about my writing so evidently it isn't so bad after all.

We had a rather hectic time last week. The dance was a great success, refreshment was ad-lib, and practically everybody was in a light-hearted mood, and nobody was drunk, much to my surprise.

Then on Sat. our land-lady held a party for us, she was really good, making plenty of cakes, sandwiches, etc, and better still, buying all the beer. We didn't pack up until 3am. I think we were too tired to carry on any longer.

Well it will not be advisable to write to this address again. I guess you know the address, but just in case, I'll write to you again later in the week when it will then be official.

The boat sure does look fine, it is really quite elaborately furnished. We should be able to keep it like it too.

Well, will close now.

Kind regards to all.

Cheerio, and all the best.
John.

It is interesting to see John speaking about both his life in the Navy, as *Turbulent* was getting closer and closer to being commissioned, as well as his personal life. The main thing that comes across in the tone of his letters is how happy and content he appears to be, despite knowing he and his colleagues are preparing to go off to war and an uncertain future.

Having been launched on 12 May 1941, HMS *Turbulent* was finally commissioned seven months later on 2 December. Despite having to undergo a period of trials at sea, the vessel had already been allocated to the 1st Submarine Flotilla, which at the time was situated at the Port of Alexandria in Egypt.

Between 2 and 7 December *Turbulent* and its crew conducted speed trials and other exercises in the River Clyde, which has some of the deepest coastal waters to be found anywhere in the British Isles. The other reason the Clyde was an ideal location to carry out such trials is that the mouth of the river is nicely sheltered from the potential ravages of the Atlantic Ocean.

The last of the letters provided by the Deller family is dated 10 October 1942, and although initially believed to have been written by John to his brother Jim, it was, in fact, the other way round.

> Dear Brother,
>
> Take note, yesterday at 11.40pm, another Deller came into the limelight. We have a son, 10lb. What a boy, eh!, and we think his name shall be John. How does that suit you? Aren't we lucky eh! I'm enclosing a small sum to wet his head, with that putrid stuff called beer. My mate came through top hole, and is now anxious to be able to dress herself up, without as she says, looking like Noah's Arc. By the way John, Pool said she does appreciate the way you folks have taken to her.

> This baby is a proper little Pakeha [a white New Zealander as opposed to a Māori] I think, and boy does he have dad's conk [nose].
>
> Lynne says she thinks there must be some Jewish in the family. Trust the underworld is still ok. Well Pal, Lynne is in the home for 14 more days, so I will get her to write to you. I have just written home.
>
> Yours affectionately
> Jim, Lynne, Wane and John.

It is believed the letter never reached John as the Postal Order for ten shillings was returned to his brother Jim, back in New Zealand, having never been cashed.

HMS *Turbulent* had begun its eighth war patrol having left Port Said on 22 September 1942, with orders to patrol off the Libyan coast, specifically in the region of Tobruk and Benghazi. It was a relatively busy patrol involving a couple of attacks on enemy convoys, resulting in the sinking of the German merchant vessel, the *Kreta*, on 8 October. The patrol ended at Beirut on 14 October 1942.

HM Submarine *Turbulent* left from Algiers on 23 February 1943, on what was to be its twelfth and final patrol, with orders to patrol the Tyrrhenian Sea, off the western coast of Italy. *Turbulent* should have finished its patrol and returned to Algiers by 23 March at the latest, but it did not make it back on time. In fact, no further contact was made after 12 March and it is unknown exactly how the submarine met its end. It was believed for a long time that *Turbulent* either fell victim to an attack by an enemy surface vessel, or an underwater mine. There is also the possibility that it was struck by enemy depth charges.

By the time *Turbulent* was lost, John Deller had been part of the crew on every single one of its war patrols. This being so, it is only right to point out that like all his colleagues who served on board, between 1 January 1942 and 1 January 1943 he had spent 254 days at sea, including 124 days submerged. John and his colleagues had to endure being hunted thirteen times by enemy vessels and had also been on the receiving end of 250 depth charges. It took a special kind of individual to be able to withstand such extremities and still be able to function properly and carry out their duties. John Deller was such a man. Having been able to include some of his letters in this book has been a true privilege.

After having received and read through many letters written by or to John Deller, there were a number of questions that needed to be asked in an effort to clarify some of the points made in certain documents.

When asked about the origins of a particular document, John Deller (son of Jim Deller, John Deller's brother) replied that it was, 'a report made by Sydney Kay, not the British National Archives'. Kay's report covers his time spent as a member of HMS *Turbulent*'s crew, beginning on Saturday, 3 January 1942 and ending on Monday, 18 January 1943 when he was admitted to St Andrew's 18th Field Hospital, Malta, with rheumatic fever after *Turbulent* had returned from its tenth war patrol. It was Kay's illness, and his subsequent admission to hospital, which saved his life. Kay's report is covered in more detail in Chapter Seven.

In relation to HMS *Turbulent*'s infamous attack on the *Nino Bixio* in 1942, which was carrying Allied POWs at the time, and his uncle's involvement in the matter, John Deller had previously made the following comment on the website www.nzhistory.govt.nz:

> A survivor of *Turbulent*, telegraphist George Svenson, went ashore prior to Turbs last mission and my uncle John Deller returned from sick bay ashore. He (George Svenson) related to me in 1983 that he decoded the message received during the recharge on the surface at midnight that the war office knew *Nino Bixio* was loaded with 3,200 Allied POWs and the 320 who were blown up in the hold were from NZ and Scotland and that the survivors swimming off the ship were left there calling for help. Luckily the ship was towed to be grounded and the remaining POWs were disembarked. He also wept saying "if it hadn't been for that Captain Bligh, all might be alive today."
>
> The crew had a fair understanding of him but also knew he was hard on the domestic targets like fishing schooners, single man boats and he always missed the big targets. This might be due to disinformation he may have received to protect the Italian capital ships for the appropriation in September 1943. In terms of the Geneva Convention, the action was illegal and immoral.

There are several questions that arise from this statement:

- Why was George Svenson not a member of the *Turbulent*'s crew on her final war patrol. Was he sick?
- Was the message he received from the War Office at "midnight" on the night before the attack, or the night after the attack on the *Nino Bixio* took place?
- Why did he refer to Linton as Captain Bligh?

- Is George Svenson saying or inferring that Linton knew the *Nino Bixio* was carrying Allied POWs?
- What did he mean by "Italian capital ships for appropriation in September 1943"?

John's response to these questions was as follows:

> The message was on the night after the attack. He referred to him as Captain Bligh because he was hard-nosed and was disliked by some of the crew. He knew before they left port that the *Sestriere* and *Nino Bixio* were to leave port and had the 11,000 Allied prisoners aboard. It was illegal to attack this shipping. My Uncle was the AB Torpedoman and George said he did the good deed and missed *Sestriere* on purpose and only hit *Bixio* on the front bow piece, which saved all the lives.
>
> I will need to concentrate some effort on this last question because the Authorities have changed the story in the past decade. Roughly, the Italian Government said if you spare our ships and men from now on, we will let you have them when the war ends. The Allied landings at Sardinia were due in 6 months or so and Italy would be out of the war by that time. So Tunisia came in to it and the Italian fleet took off to Tunisia, but turned back after the deal was made.
>
> George [Svenson] wept and said those bastards in Rugby [GCHQ] knew the two vessels carried our men and he said at times he was on deck and saw many

men crying for help. It's almost impossible to write the truth for reasons of obvious clarity, however you can quote me as to what he said to me because I do not trade in untruths and George would want me to tell it as he explained.

Every night at midnight George went up to the conning tower deck to empty the trash cans and point the aerial towards Rugby to report and receive orders which were given to the boss. If you examine the sinkings, which were considerable, the boss dodged the difficult targets and many other people have criticised him for that.

The post steamer *Mafaldo* was under a free French flag and was exempt from attack but the boss wanted to get more sinkings to elevate his chances of being promoted to higher position on land after *Turbulent* was decommissioned.

He attacked a neutral vessel and it backfired. When I was in La Spezia the naval experts qualified that a man living (an unnamed Italian sailor) witnessed the attack and action and it was well known she was hit by Teti II.

This reply prompted more questions:

- John Deller stated the War Office knew *Nino Bixio* was carrying Allied POWs, but did not inform *Turbulent* until midnight, which was after the attack, the same message that George decoded. Yet at the same time Linton apparently knew that *Sestriere* and *Nino Bixio* had 11,000 Allied prisoners on board, before he left Port Said. This is further confused when his uncle, John Deller, who was a torpedoman, purposely missed the *Sestriere*. It would not have been down to him when to fire the torpedo, but Linton. This also suggests that Linton and his crew were aware that the *Sestriere* and *Nino Bixio* were carrying Allied POWs. Did Linton and his crew know they were attacking two ships that were carrying Allied POWs, before they carried out the attack? If so, why would they do that?

- If George and his colleagues saw Allied POWs in the water after they had attacked the two ships, why did they not try to rescue them?
- When was the agreement made between the Italians and the British not to attack Italian ships, and who on the British side was this deal done with?

John's response was as follows:

> Yes, they knew when the 2 ships were leaving and their orders were only relating to attack the 2 ships. George felt very strongly about this decision and told my Uncle John. I cannot say others knew the details as I was not informed, but I suppose it was kept quiet as George was responsible and some of the officers were good boys. The Boss knew they were attacking the ships because George had passed the message to him.
>
> Why did he proceed with it? Because he would get a result. Also, they were in port nearby and left

> simultaneously with the 2 ships which were only escorted by 2 destroyers. They had nothing else on their list.
>
> John was a hard case, a tough man, 23 years of age, popular, and well-known for gymnastic high diving from a capital ship's mast crosstree anytime they were in port, and I have seen the photos.
>
> George said they were not permitted to take survivors from the sea as this endangered the sub and there were too many to accommodate.
>
> It would be possible for the torpedo man to miss the target as it was manual and the time to fire was not necessarily well co-ordinated with the firer. The full crew would not have gone along with it if they knew what the ships were carrying.

Taken at face value, John Deller's account of what took place, and the part HMS *Turbulent* and members of its crew played in it, as related to him by George Svenson, is extremely compelling. Is it plausible? Most definitely. Is this what actually happened? More than likely, but the only person who knows for certain is George Svenson, but as he is no longer with us and because John Deller would have nothing to gain from making such claims, it can only be assumed to be factual.

Questions still remained, however. When did George Svenson receive the message from GCHQ that the *Nino Bixio* and the other vessel were carrying POWs? Was it midnight before the day of the attack, or midnight on the day of the attack? If the message was in fact received the midnight before, why did they then carry out the attack knowing there were Allied POWs on board who would be killed?

John Deller replied by saying that:

> George stated they were in port and he received the message in port. He said clearly that those bastards knew what the 2 vessels were transporting because the port where they embarked was teeming with spies working for them, and as I said, he wept saying that if it had not been for that Captain Bligh, they would all still be alive.

The letters written by John Deller act as a small window into the life of a submariner in the Second World War. It is almost as if they were part of a cathartic escape for him from the rigours of a wartime existence, the claustrophobic life on board a submarine, and the continued separation from his loved ones.

The letters in the main are light-hearted and about family related matters, although in the letter dated 11 November 1941, he does provide certain information to his brother about the workings of HMS *Turbulent*, but stops short of providing too much detail.

In addition the letters, John Deller was also given the following notes and observations by the Italian naval base at La Spezia. Originally in Italian, Deller subsequently had them translated into English. Large sections of these handwritten notes were legible, but some parts were not. In each such instance, the author has included the most obvious interpretation of what is implied.

There is no date on the translated notes, but the original Italian version allegedly includes information provided by an unnamed witness to the attack on the *Nino Bixio*. However, it has not been possible to establish if this witness was a crew member from the stricken vessel or the *Sestriere*.

The references in the notes to a "SUB" strongly suggests that the submarine in question on each occasion was, in fact, *Turbulent*.

> *Turbulent* continued to a position south-east of Sardinia. On its arrival, it should have made contact with its operational command.
>
> This contact did not happen, and the vessel did not return to its base. It can be added that the average duration of the missions of the subs of the class to which the TURBULENT belonged, were in the region of 20 days.
>
> It is very possible that the vessel was expected in Algiers around the middle of March.
>
> From the national sources of information listed below we learned the following:
>
> Diary of Supermarina of 1 March.
>
> At 09:45, in the vicinity of Paola [Malta] an enemy SUB launched a torpedo attack against the ship S.VINCENZO of 865 tons, which was en route between Naples and Milazzo [Sicily]. The torpedo explodes on the beach. The SUB surfaces and fires its guns at the vessel hitting it several times.

The coastal defences of Paola opens fire and forces the SUB to submerge. The SUB fires another torpedo that hits the ship, sinking it at 10:00 at 1 mile from the observation point at Paola.

The DEZZA performs a search from 12:20 to 10:40 the next day without any success.

A navigation report from the ARDITO in relation to a convoy of three steamers escorted by five torpedo boats despatched from Naples on 6 March 1943, and directed to TRAPANI [Sicily].

07:45 hours on 6 March at 34 miles from Punta Licosa near Salerno, a JU 88 drops a depth charge bomb at the stern of my ship at approximately 3,000 metres.

I immediately give directions for an attack whilst the convoy turns to the left, the aircraft continues its flight path to the point of visual contact.

The ECG [Sonar] beats an echo at 1,300 meters from source. I get closer and launch the first WBD [Depth Charge], turn round and return to the point where I had heard the signal.

The ECG signals an echo at 1,000 meters. I enter the collision course to launch a second depth charge with the echo at 600 meters from source.

I am over the point and about to launch, when due to low pressure in the tanks, the ship loses speed

> suddenly, making it impossible, for reasons of safety, to launch the bombs. I halt the attack and move to a distance to return to the point where I launched a second signal to start a second attack.
>
> From the report, we do not know how many attacks were effected and how many bombs were launched. We only know that at 09:35 contact was lost without anything being noted, which could make the captain of the ARDITO think he had hit the SUB.

While this report may not necessarily provide any additional information about the attack on the *Nino Bixio* that has not already been discussed earlier, it does provide detail of the subsequent attempts by the escorting vessels tasked with protecting the *Nino Bixio* and the *S.Vincenzo* to attack and destroy HMS *Turbulent.* If accepted as an honest and truthful account of those events, and there is no reason to believe otherwise, it shows the speed at which the Italian escort vessels responded to the attack. The period immediately afterwards was extremely difficult for *Turbulent* and its crew as it had to be able to dive as quickly as possible in order to prevent the escorting vessels from accurately dropping their depth charges.

CHAPTER SIX

Report by George Svenson – Telegraphist on board HMS *Turbulent*

The following are extracts taken from a typed diary-style report made by George Svenson, a crew member and telegraphist who served on board HM Submarine *Turbulent* up until, and including, the vessel's eleventh and penultimate war patrol. Svenson would undoubtedly have been on that ill-fated twelfth and fateful patrol if he had not been struck down with jaundice.

As mentioned in the previous chapter, the diary came to be in the possession of Mr John Deller, the nephew of 25-year-old Able Seaman 1st Class, John Albert Deller, who dies when *Turbulent* went missing in March 1943.

The entries cover the period between January 1942 and 12 March 1943. Additional comments and observations interspersed between the entries have been provided to provide further information to the original text.

1942

> January 1942, saw that in the general picture of submarine activities, little had changed except for a partial re-occupation of the areas off the east coast of Tunisia by the 10th Flotilla. The overall rate of sinkings dropped, but the tonnage of damaged ships was maintained. Against this, three U-boats, one German and two Italian, were sunk by our submarines. One British submarine was lost, *Triumph* (Lieutenant J. S. Huddart).

HMS *Triumph* was a T-class submarine which, at the outbreak of the Second World War, was part of the Royal Navy's 2nd Submarine Flotilla, collectively stationed at bases at Dundee, in Scotland, and Blyth, in Northumberland. It was lost sometime in January 1942, along with all fifty-nine members of its crew, somewhere in the Aegean Sea, off the coast of Greece.

First commissioned in May 1939, it had an extremely lucky escape when striking a German mine in the North Sea on 26 December 1939. The explosion ripped 18 feet from its bow section, but remarkably, it stayed afloat and made it back to base with the assistance of an escort. It took nine months to complete the required repairs and it was 27 September 1940 before *Triumph* was back in the water. Once operational again, *Triumph* was used in a number of covert operations, dropping off and picking up Allied agents along the Greek coast. It left base at Alexandria on 26 December 1941 to conduct a war patrol in the Aegean Sea. It never returned. To date, the submarine's location on the seabed has not been discovered.

Its commander, Lieutenant John Symons Huddart, had served on submarines since 1 January 1934, his first posting being on HMS *Orpehus* in January 1935. HMS *Triumph* was the sixth submarine of the war Huddart had served on, becoming its commanding officer on 8 November 1941.

At the time of *Triumph's* disappearance, the vessel was on its twenty-first war patrol.

> **January** – [*Turbulent*] Arrived at Gibraltar, as a brand new boat carried out working-up patrols preparatory to joining the 1st submarine Flotilla, taking the place of *Trusty* and *Truant*, who had left at the end of December 1941 for the Far East.
>
> **January** – Spent the early part of the month on passage from Gibraltar to Alexandria via Malta carrying stores and equipment for the two submarine flotillas.
>
> **February 23** – Left Alexandria for a patrol in the Aegean with a roving commission.
>
> **February 26** – An unsuccessful attack on a convoy off Suda Bay.

At just after 0800 hours on 26 February, HMS *Turbulent* spotted three Axis anti-submarine trawlers leaving Suda Bay, Crete, which then headed north. Commander Linton decided to follow them, but not attack; a decision which hours later proved to be the right one. At just after 1430 hours, about 10 miles north of Suda Bay, the three trawlers met up with three merchant ships that were being escorted by four destroyers and four patrol boats, with a number of aircraft in the skies above providing additional protection. Linton decided it was time to begin his attack, but this was a mistake. At just before 1300 hours, *Turbulent* was spotted by one of the convoy's escorts, who quickly manoeuvred into position before dropping depth charges, which it managed to do before *Turbulent* could fire any of its torpedoes. Luckily, *Turbulent* was not damaged in the attack and managed to slip away.

The convoy and its escort vessels included the following ships: the Italian liners *Citta di Agrigento, Citta di Alessandri* and the *Citta di Savona*, along with the German merchant vessel, and they were escorted by the German auxiliary vessel *Drache* and the Italian torpedo boats *Monzambano and Castelfidardo.* As well as these ships there were also four trawlers and the German patrol-boats *12 V 6, 12 V 7 and 12 V 4*. It was the latter of these vessels which spotted and depth charged *Turbulent.*

February 27 – A caique was sunk by gunfire.

On 27 February HMS *Turbulent* sank the Greek caique Pi 253/ *Agios Charalambos* (a comparatively small vessel at only 68 gross tonnes), just north of Monemvasia, Greece. Rather than waste a valuable torpedo, the attack was carried out with the use of the submarine's deck gun.

HMS *Turbulent* first sighted the caique at approximately 1430 hours, but it was more than an hour later before the submarine surfaced and, at a distance of about 3,000 yards, opened fire on the unsuspecting Greek vessel flying its national flag.

The caique was heavily laden and had a large cargo visible on its deck, along with at least forty members of crew. Once the vessel had seen *Turbulent*, it tried its best to escape, but to no avail. The caique altered course numerous times and was difficult to hit; by the time the attack was over, *Turbulent* had fired a total of forty-two rounds, of which only six managed to hit the target, although this was sufficient to sink it.

A minute after *Turbulent* sank the caique at 1548 hours, it dived back below the waves.

> **March 2** – Patrol was then shifted to the Gulf of Salonika via the Doro Channel. Three schooners were sunk by gunfire followed by a fourth.

> **April 5** – In the Adriatic *Turbulent* lived up to her name. Passing through the Strait of Otranto.

Named after the Italian city of Taranto, the Strait of Otranto separates Italy from Albania and has been of strategic importance since Roman times. The most easterly point of Italy at Punta Palascia, just east of Salento, is only 45 miles from the Albanian coast. It also connects the Adriatic Sea with the Ionian Sea.

> **April 7** – Started the first Adriatic war patrol by sinking the *Rosa M.* (271 tons) by gunfire.

The *Rosa M* was an Italian merchant vessel travelling from Gravosa to Durazzo, in Croatia, when it was attacked by HMS *Turbulent* and sunk 7 miles south of the coastal town of Petrovac.

> **April 9** – Unsuccessful torpedo attack was carried out on a 3,000-ton ship off Sibenik.

> **April 10** – Unsuccessful torpedo attack off Ortona.

> **April 12** – A U-boat of the Balilla class avoided destruction off Fiume by a timely alteration of course.
>
> **April 13** – A steamer was fired at and missed.
>
> **April 14** – Returning to the Sibenik area, engaged two schooners by gunfire but was only able to damage one of them before being forced to dive by return fire from the shore batteries.

The shore battery in question was situated within the walls of the sixteenth-century St Nicholas Fortress, built by the Venetians to prevent Turkish naval attacks and amphibious landings from taking place.

> **April 15** – Approaching to within 1 mile of Dubrovnik harbour, it proved to be empty of shipping.

At the time, Dubrovnik and its harbour were occupied by the Italians. This continued until 8 September 1943, when, after Italy surrendered to the Allies, it was then occupied by elements of the German Army.

> **April 16** – Monopoli on the Italian coast provided better results, the unescorted *Delia* (5,404 tons) heavily laden and southbound, being sunk by torpedo.

The *Delia* was an Italian cargo ship, built in 1917 for the British-owned Tatem Steam Navigation Company, and initially had the name of SS *Buckleigh.* In 1923, the vessel was sold to an Italian shipping company who renamed her the SS *Valfiorta.* It was in 1935, after having been purchased by Industrie Navali Sa, of Genoa, that the *Valfiorta* became the *Delia.*

The *Delia* was attacked by HM Submarine *Turbulent* 3 miles off Villanova, near Brindisi, whilst en route to Taranto.

April 17 – Left the Adriatic and returned to base at Alexandria.

April 23 – Arriving at Alexandria.

Turbulent's first patrol lasted for two months, during which time it was involved in ten attacks and sank seven enemy vessels. After a break of eighteen days, during which time the submarine was refuelled, mechanically checked over, re-stocked with supplies and munitions, and its crew given a well-deserved rest, it left its base at Alexandria to begin its second patrol.

May 11 – Left Alexandria for patrol in the Gulf of Sirte.

May 14 – Two out of three schooners attacked by gunfire were destroyed before the submarine was put down by enemy aircraft off Ras el Hilal.

May 16 – Reached the Benghazi area, suffering a good deal of interference from aircraft patrols.

May 17 – A convoy sighted in the evening and, after patient shadowing, was able to work ahead of the quarry and torpedo the *Bolsena* (2,384 tons) in the early hours of the following morning.

The *Bolsena* was torpedoed by *Turbulent* north of Benghazi. As in the case of SS *Delia,* the *Bolsena* was also built in England, at Sunderland, Tyne & Weir.

> **May 18** – Inaccurate reports from our aircraft led to another convoy being missed.
>
> **May 24** – Low surface speed of the T-class submarines was the cause of another convoy getting past unscathed.
>
> **May 26** – Another convoy got clear, *Turbulent* being sighted and forced to dive by the escort during a night attack.
>
> **May 29** – At 0020 a convoy was sighted and shadowed in order to carry out a dawn attack. Four hours later four torpedoes were fired. One hit and sank the *Capo Arma* (3,172 tons) while another ran wild after passing over *Turbulent.* Sank the large Italian destroyer *Pessagno* (1,917 tons).

The *Capo Arma,* a British-built cargo vessel but owned by an Italian shipping company based in Genoa, was struck by a single torpedo approximately 70 miles north-west of Benghazi.

The *Pessagno*, also known as RM *Emanuele Pessagno*, was hit and sunk some 85 miles north-west of Benghazi by two torpedoes fired by *Turbulent* at 0330 hours. One struck the bow whilst the other hit amidships, sinking the vessel in less than one minute. Out of a crew of 225, only 85 survived.

> **June 2** – Started on return journey, meeting *U-81* but failed to hit her in two attacks.

The German *Kriegsmarine* submarine *U-81* was a type VIIC U-boat. At 220 feet 2 inches in length, it was bigger than the type VIIB submarines that preceded it, and, somewhat remarkably, could operate at depths of up to 750 feet. Its maximum surface speed was 17.7 knots, which was just over 20 miles per hour. *U-81* had five torpedo tubes and an additional arsenal of one 8.8cm naval gun, as well as an anti-aircraft gun.

It was commissioned on 26 April 1941 as part of the 1st U-boat Flotilla and first set to sea under the command of Oberleutnant zur See Friedrich Guggenberger.

U-81 had a lucky escape when it was attacked by aircraft of the Royal Air Force's No. 209 Squadron on 30 October 1941 while attempting to cross the Strait of Gibraltar on its way to the Mediterranean. After being hit by aerial depth charges, it slowly made its way back to its home port of Brest, on the west coast of France, to have the damage repaired. The journey was not without its dangers because due to the severity of the damage, *U-81* had to remain on the surface all the way. Remarkably, just four days after arriving at Brest, *U-81* had been repaired and had set off again en route for La Spezia in Italy.

On 13 November 1941, approximately 30 miles from Gibraltar, *U-81* attacked HMS *Ark Royal*, an aircraft carrier of the British Royal Navy. After being hit by a single torpedo, *Ark Royal* sank the next day before it could be towed into Gibraltar.

The missed opportunity by HMS *Turbulent* to sink *U-81* was to come at a price. Between 10 November 1942 and 18 November 1943, *U-81* attacked and sank a total of fifteen

Allied vessels of different types and weights, as well as damaging two others.

The end for *U-81* came on 9 January 1944, when it was attacked by American bomber aircraft at its home base of Pola, Croatia.

> **June 4** – Arrived in Alexandria. Commander Linton made urgent representations as to possible improvements in co-operation between aircraft and submarines, with the result that an experienced submarine officer was appointed for liaison duties with the R.A.F. A similar arrangement had been adopted some months previously in home waters.
>
> **June 17** – Left Alexandria for the Gulf of Sirte.
>
> **June 22** – Attacked and sank a small escorted steamer [unidentified].
>
> **June 24** – The Italian *Regulus* (1,085 tons), also escorted, was torpedoed and sunk.

The *Regulus* was an Italian steam freighter en route from Tripoli to Benghazi.

> The events of May and June merge into one phase. During the early part of May, submarines of the 1st Flotilla operated in the Adriatic and in the Gulf of Sirte. Towards the end of this month and during June the provision of cover for Malta convoys from the west and from the east occupied most of the available submarine strength.

The situation on shore had deteriorated badly by mid-June; so much in fact that arrangements were made for the orderly retirement of the Fleet to Port Said and Haifa. To the eastward of Malta both the 1st and 10th Flotillas kept up their pressure on the North African convoys running down the west coast of Greece to Benghazi.

July 4 – No further contacts with the enemy were made until today when an attempt to attack a convoy of three ships was thwarted by the attentions of the air and surface escort. The resultant bombing and depth charging, though very heavy, did not deter Commander Linton from a study of zoology. He recorded in his patrol reports that; "The noise appeared to excite the amorous instincts of the rats; throughout the afternoon there were shrill screams of satisfaction behind the three-ply above my bunk."

July 8 – Moved across to Tobruk.

July 14 – A brief glimpse of a U-boat.

July 15 – Had no further sightings before arriving at Beirut.

August 5 – Left Beirut.

August 8 – Recovered an agent from south-west corner of Crete.

August 11 – Landed two other agents near Navarin on the night of 11th/12th.

The agents in question would have been part of the Special Operations Executive (SOE), which helped the resistance movement on Crete. These included individuals such as archaeologist John Pendulbury, who was known as "the Cretan Lawrence", a reference to Lawrence of Arabia. Others included writer and adventurer Patrick Leigh Fermor and Ivan William Stanley Moss, more commonly known as W. Stanley Moss, a British Army Officer in the Cold Stream Guards and best known for kidnapping the German General Heinrich Kreipe.

August 16 – After operating off Argostoli and Zante, proceeded to the AntiKythera channel but turned back on receipt of intelligence that a convoy was expected off the Greek coast.

August 17 – Northbound convoy of two large ships with destroyer and air escort was successfully intercepted and attacked, the 7,000 ton ship *Nino Bixio* being hit with two torpedoes; in spite of this the vessel was successfully towed into Navarin.

August 19 – Patrol off the south-west corner of Crete from 19th to 27th, yielded no targets.

August 27 – Leaving patrol.

September 1 – Arrive at Beirut.

September 22 – Left Port Said. After a period of 24 hours off the south-west coast of Crete, arrived off Tobruk on the 27th, but was shortly ordered to patrol in the Benghazi approaches.

During September 1942, the volume of Axis shipping sunk by our submarines in the Mediterranean fell sharply, while the claims to have damaged ships rose in proportion. The actual results of these latter claims cannot be fully verified from Axis records and many of the claims are based on estimates, as the much-improved Axis anti-submarine technique prevented submarines from seeing the result of their shots. The reason for this lack of success was largely that the increase in efficiency of the Axis anti-submarine forces made it necessary to send our submarines to patrol in widely dispersed areas so as to prevent the Axis Command from concentrating anti-surface forces in the most vital areas, some of which, notably the Gulf of Taranto, were proving too well guarded for our submarines to be able to operate effectively. This policy of dispersed attack was fully justified as shown in Axis records. As far back as April 1942 ships were held in port through lack of escorts, while in July transport flights by the Italian air force were suspended owing to the necessity, inter alia, of providing anti-submarine escorts and patrols. On 14 September, by which time Mussolini had already stated that the sea war in the Mediterranean had been lost, the crisis in the Axis Panzer Army supply situation was stated by the Axis Command to be due to the following causes: (a) shortage of shipping space; (b) difficulties in providing convoy escorts. Much of this was caused by our successful submarine campaign, but by the autumn of 1942 our increasing air strength and the consequent intensification of our air warfare against the Axis supply lines was causing the Axis more concern than the submarine attacks. The bulk of the work, however, had already been done by the steady drain caused by our submarine campaign of the past two years.

Patrols off the North African coast between Benghazi and Tobruk were maintained during September 1942 by the 1st Flotilla with a fair degree of success.

October 2 – Sighted a tanker too far off to attack.

October 6 – Missed one convoy.

October 7 – Missed another convoy.

October 8 – Sank the German supply ship *Kreta* (2,359 tons).

The *Kreta*, which had formerly been the French ship the SS *Ile de Beaute*, had been captured by the Germans and subsequently used as an aircraft support vessel. There is some confusion about how it met its actual end, with some claiming it was sunk by HM Submarine *Unseen* on 21 September 1943, nearly a year after what is recorded in *Turbulent*'s War Diary. As with the mystery surrounding the loss of HMS *Turbulent*, there were many occasions during the war where confusion and uncertainty were common in relation to the loss of both submarine and surface vessels. The two main reasons for this were the inability by an attacking vessel to be able to identify with certainty the vessel they were attacking, and the fact that both the Allies and Axis nations did not want to confirm the number of losses that they had sustained in any attack.

The website www.uboat.net, which includes entries from *Unseen*'s War Diary, indicate that the submarine did, in fact, sink the *Kreta* at 1740 hours on 21 September 1943.

> **October 10** – Nothing further sighted, left patrol.
>
> **October 14** – Arrived at Beirut.

Svenson goes on to give further information regarding the situation for the Axis powers:

> Before dealing with the submarine operations in direct support of the Allied landings, it is interesting to record something of the Axis side of the picture. As early as June 1942 the Axis started preparations to occupy the French Mediterranean coast in the event of an Allied attempt to land in southern France. Consideration was also given to the Italian aspirations to occupy Tunis and Bizerta, the former having a large Italian population.
>
> The Axis High Command were apparently aware in July 1942 that the Allies were preparing something for North Africa, but opinion differed as to the scope and area of these plans. The Germans, even as late as mid-October, believed that the Allies intended to land in French West Africa, but discounted the possibility of an attack on Mediterranean coasts.

This was not the Italian opinion, which tended towards Algiers and Oran. In any case the Axis, or at least the German end of it, assumed that the defence of French Africa was a French commitment which Vichy France would live up to.

Mussolini was not so certain about this, rightly divining that politically, the North African landings would be placed under American aegis, France having no quarrel with that country. The Axis preparations for the occupation of Tunisia had not got beyond the discussion stage when the Allies struck, but the landings at Algiers and Oran made early action imperative.

Making a virtue of necessity, the Vichy French Government put their Tunisian bases at the disposal of the Axis on 9 November, this gesture being rewarded by German troops occupying the whole of Southern France two days later.

Operation Torch, the Allied invasion of French North Africa, which began on 8 November 1942, was actually more about attempting to draw Axis forces away from the Eastern Front and relieving the pressure on hard pressed Soviet forces, than it was an actual Allied desire to invade North Africa.

Part of Operation Torch involved Royal Navy submarines operating in the Mediterranean Sea so as to prevent elements of the Italian Navy from interfering with the Allied invasion. To this end, the *Turbulent, Traveller, Parthian, Porpoise,* and the

Rorqual transferred from the 1st Submarine Flotilla to the greatly augmented 10th Submarine Flotilla. Out of the twenty-seven submarines at the Flotilla's disposal, thirteen of them sailed from Malta between 1 and 3 November, with the *Parthian* and the *Turbulent* bringing up the rear.

This type of submarine was chosen for the job for specific reasons. They were slow in comparison to other classes of submarine, and gave off a relatively small silhouette. These two elements made them ideal for inshore patrols. As part of Operation Torch, the submarine Flotillas were told not to attack enemy convoys until 2100 hours on 11 November, after which time, they were free to carry out attacks as they saw fit to do so.

The operation's naval tactics were a total success and went some way to making sure that the Italian naval Fleet, chose not to interfere with the Allied invasion of North Africa, ensuring that the infantry men who came ashore did so unopposed, allowing them to quickly gain a foothold.

November 4 – Left Malta.

November 5 – *Turbulent* was in its initial patrol position by dawn, on a line south-eastward from Cavoli Light, which was on the south-east corner of Sardinia.

News of the successful Allied landings was received by *Turbulent*, as well as the crews of other submarines in the Mediterranean, late on the morning of 8 November. Fortunately, there was no attempt by Axis submarines and naval vessels to retaliate against Allied submarines, but this was more a practical decision than anything else. By now the Italian Fleet was hampered by fuel shortages and a lack of air and surface escorts. The only action the Italians did take was to move their battleships from Taranto to Naples, which fortunately for them went completely undetected by British reconnaissance and intelligence forces, not to mention potential attacks from *Turbulent* and other submarines in the area.

> **November 11** – Attacked a north bound ship bound for Cagliari; one torpedo hit right aft and the ship sank. This was the 1,554-ton German ship *Benghazi*, which before its capture had been the Danish vessel, the *Almera*, which had only recently been converted to be a German U-boat depot ship at Cagliari and was carrying, amongst other important supplies, forty new type electric torpedoes, much needed supplies of fuel, lubricating oil and twelve months' stores, rations and provisions for the region's German U-boat contingent.
>
> The sinking of the *Benghazi* annoyed the German authorities immensely as supplies of any kind were extremely hard to come by in the Mediterranean, and also because they had no suitable vessel as an obvious and immediate replacement.

At noon the commanders of the 10th Submarine Flotilla received orders to redeploy their vessels in an effort to prevent Axis vessels from reaching the ports at Bizerta and along the length of the Eastern Tunisian coastline. The ultimate part of the plan was to trap the Italian Fleet at sea, should they decide to leave the relative safety of their ports.

Things did not quite go according to plan for the British as a number of vessels of the Italian Fleet made it out to sea unnoticed. Three cruisers left the Port of Augusta, but then somewhat unexpectedly headed north towards Messina, all the while staying as close to the coastline as they could safely do so without running aground. In the meantime, three *Littorio*-class battleships quietly slipped out of the Port of Taranto heading for Naples. In no rush, instead they proceeded at a leisurely pace in an effort to preserve fuel. Amazingly their "escape" from Taranto was not even noticed by the British until the morning of 12 November.

HMS *Turbulent* had been sent north with its intended destination being Naples in an effort to stop the Italian battleships from reaching the port there. There was confusion as to what speed the Italian vessels were travelling at, meaning calculations as to an estimated time of arrival at Naples were wrong and *Turbulent* did not arrive in time to prevent the battleships from reaching the safety of the port some 10 miles ahead.

Once again, Svenson provides further commentary as to what happened next:

> Thus after the first four days of the start of '[Operation] Torch', our submarines were, to all intents and purposes back to their pre-Torch duties of harrying all Axis seaborne supply lines in the Mediterranean with special emphasis on the campaign in North Africa. To this end the Naval Commander, Expeditionary Force, on 14 November

requested the Admiralty to extend the Sink at Sight zone in the Mediterranean to the whole Western Mediterranean Basin, except Spanish territorial waters (including reasonable access to the Balearic Islands). The Admiralty were prompt in their reply, which was made on 17 November, and went even further than they had been asked to go.

From 0800 hours on 21 November all waters in the Mediterranean, excluding Turkish territorial waters, were declared dangerous to shipping east of the line from the Franco-Spanish border along the edge of Spanish territorial waters to a point 3 miles 090 degrees from Cape de Creus (42 degrees 19' N., 03 degrees 19' E.), through position 39 degrees 46'N., 04 degrees 50' E., thence 180 degrees to the Algerian coast.

For political reasons it was desired to give the Spanish as much sea room as possible, as in future the Allies might wish to encourage a measure of trade between Spain and Algeria. As a temporary measure, south- and west-bound French ships were not to be attacked west of a line drawn from Cape de Creus to the Algerian coast, outside the new Sink on Sight zone.

During this second phase of Operation Torch from 12 November to 12 December, our submarines experienced one of the most unsuccessful periods of the war, particularly in the vital area between Palermo and Tunis.

The discussion as to which was more important for a submarine commander to achieve, overall tonnage or the number of vessels sunk, is an interesting one. The main purpose of submarines in wartime is to attack and destroy enemy shipping, whether they be naval or merchant vessels. Because of the continuous importation of food stuffs, military equipment and soldiers making their way across the Atlantic Ocean, merchant vessels became an obvious target for German U-boats. They were also easier targets because unless they were part of a well-protected convoy, they had no real capability of defending themselves. According to figures supplied by the Admiralty after the war, a total of 2,548 Allied merchant vessels were lost, of which 2,246 were as a direct result of enemy action.

Ultimately, it was the submarine's commander who decided which vessels his submarine would attack, with personal achievement and glory sometimes acting as their main driving force.

To help with this, it is perhaps useful to compare different commanders' "achievements".

Benjamin Bryant CB DSO (Two Bars) DSC MiD, who ended his service in the Royal Navy with the rank of Rear Admiral, was the most successful British submarine commander to have survived the Second World War, based on the number of enemy vessels sunk. His tally was twenty-seven sunk as well as nine damaged, many of which beyond repair, but for Bryant those numbers were not sufficient to obtain a Victoria Cross. The number of enemy vessels he could have sunk might well have been much higher: in total, a staggering sixty-seven of the torpedoes he fired missed their targets.

John Linton VC DSO DSC joined the Royal Navy in 1926 as an Acting Sub-Lieutenant. By the beginning of the Second World War he had reached the rank of Commander, and in April 1940 was put in command of the submarine HMS *Pandora*. Having arrived in Malta on 31 March 1942 to unload its stores, a bombing raid by the Luftwaffe took place on 1 April while it was still being unloaded. Despite the obvious dangers, the decision was taken to continue with the unloading to save time. *Pandora* took two direct bomb hits and was sunk.

Linton was *Turbulent's* first and only commander and was in charge when the submarine left the shipping yard at Barrow on 31 November 1941. His war time service saw him receive recognition of his efforts: he was awarded the Distinguished Service Cross on 6 May 1941, the Distinguished Service Order on 15 September 1942, and the Victoria Cross on 25 May 1943, some two months after his death. In total, Linton commanded submarines that sank thirty-one enemy vessels with a combined weight of more than 90,000 tons.

Malcolm David Wanklyn VC DSO (Two Bars) commanded submarines that in total sank seventeen enemy vessels, damaged six others, and destroyed another with charges. In total these enemy vessels weighed 128,353 tons. Lieutenant Commander Wanklyn commanded HM Submarine *Upholder* when the vessel and crew were lost on 14 April 1942, while on patrol in the Mediterranean Sea.

November 22 – Making a passage from Malta to Beirut, did a short patrol along the North African coast, but was only able to bombard a car park near Sirte.

December 23 – After a brief rest at Beirut, returned on loan to the 10th Flotilla, arriving at Malta on 23 December.

December 26 – Left Malta to begin her next patrol.

December 29 – Off Cavoli Island, east of Cape Ferrato, Sardinia, torpedoed and sank the Italian merchant steamer *Marte* (5,290 tons).

December 30 – Moved up the east coast of Sardinia to reconnoitre and report on the vicinity of Maddalena. This information was required for [Operation] Chariot operations being carried out early in the new year. *Turbulent* then made for the Capri area but encountered very heavy weather for the next few days and saw no targets.

1943

January 8 – Formed a patrol line with *Una* (Lieutenant J. D. Martin) and *United* (Lieutenant J.C.Y. Roxburgh) south of Capri in the expectation of intercepting a convoy.

HMS *Una* was a U-class submarine that survived the war before being decommissioned in November 1945 and sold for scrap on 11 April 1949. The submarine's commander at the time was Lieutenant John Dennis Martin, who remained in charge until 29 April 1943. *Una* had left Malta to begin its eighteenth war patrol on 4 January.

HMS *United* survived the war and was decommissioned into the naval reserve on 22 October 1945, before being scrapped at Troon on 12 February 1946.

The commander of HMS *United*, Lieutenant John Charles Young Roxburgh DSO DSC (Bar), survived the war and went on to reach the exulted rank of Vice Admiral, finally retiring in October 1972, having served for thirty-three years.

> **January 9** – Hopes were not realised and the patrol line was discontinued.

> **January 11** – Closed the coast off Paola, sank the *Vittoria Beraldo* (547 tons) by a combination of gun and torpedo fire. The same day a train north of San Lucido station received severe treatment at the hands of the gun crew, after which the submarine left patrol for Malta.

The *Vittoria Beraldo* was an Italian motor cargo vessel sailing just 200 metres off Capo Testa, near Cetrato, en route from Scario to Vibo Valentia, when it was sunk.

> **January 25** – Left Malta to patrol off the north-west coast of Sicily.

> **January 27** – Fired four torpedoes at one of two ships under escort; one torpedo hit and damaged a 3,000 ton steamer. In the next few days targets passed out of range.

The vessel in question was part of a convoy which included the Italian merchant ships *Spoleto* and *Noto*, who were escorted by two Italian destroyers and a torpedo boat.

British submarines out of Malta and Algiers, which included *Turbulent*, carried out patrols along the Sicilian coastline during the months of January and February 1943. Their job was to try to intercept any Axis vessels attempting to enter the Port of Tunis.

> **January 31** – Had to go deep, while attacking two eastbound ships in ballast, to avoid the screen.

February 1 – The merchant ship *Pozzuoli* (5,350 tons) was seen to sink after being hit by two torpedoes fired at her. A Ramb class A.M.C. [Armed Merchant Cruiser], followed up, stopped in the vicinity. A stern torpedo was fired at her but she went ahead just before it got there and the torpedo missed. Several e-boats appeared but did not inconvenience *Turbulent.*

February 2 – Unable to attack four destroyers who passed in the evening owing to bad light.

February 5 – The 5,340-ton Italian fuel tanker *Utilitas* was sunk at dawn with two hits out of four torpedoes fired, some 15 miles east of Palermo, Sicily, en route from Taranto to Palermo, despite being escorted by a destroyer and torpedo boats.

It was not uncommon for fuel tankers of the size of the *Utilitas* to be carrying somewhere in the region of 100 tons of fuel. Having been struck by two torpedoes, if the *Utilitas*'s cargo had ignited, the subsequent explosion and fireball that followed would have quite literally blown the ship to pieces and vaporised anybody on board.

February 7 – A train in St Ambroglio station, near Cefalu, was the target for *Turbulent*'s guns at a distance of over 2,000 metres, several hits being observed, which wrecked the train and a number of its wagons, although the train track remained intact.

That night *Turbulent* was hunted and depth-charged by E-boats, without any recorded damage.

John Philip Holland, the Irish engineer who designed and developed the first Royal Navy submarine, *Holland 1*.

HMS *Turbulent* in Malta harbour.

HMS *Turbulent*, with her 'Jolly Roger' clearly displayed, seen returning to Malta after a war patrol.

An example of life on board a wartime submarine.

Conditions on board all submarines, including *Turbulent*, were extremely cramped. Space was at a premium.

A group of *Turbulent*'s crew on deck with their 'Jolly Roger' flag.

Turbulent's full crew on deck after returning from a war patrol.

A 4-inch (102 mm) deck gun was standard on all Royal Navy submarines during the Second World War, including HMS *Turbulent*.

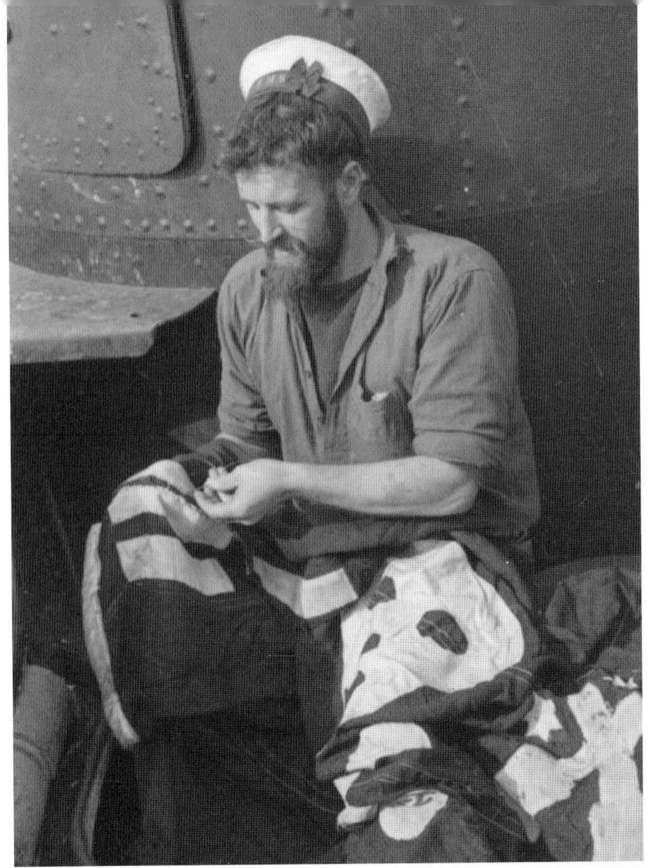

A crew member making an addition to the submarine's 'Jolly Roger'.

HMS *Turbulent* refuelling in Malta before leaving on another Mediterranean war patrol.

John Linton, HMS *Turbulent*'s only commander.

John Linton and his wife, Nancy.

HMS *Pandora* was John Linton's command before he was assigned to HMS *Turbulent*.

John Linton in slightly relaxed pose.

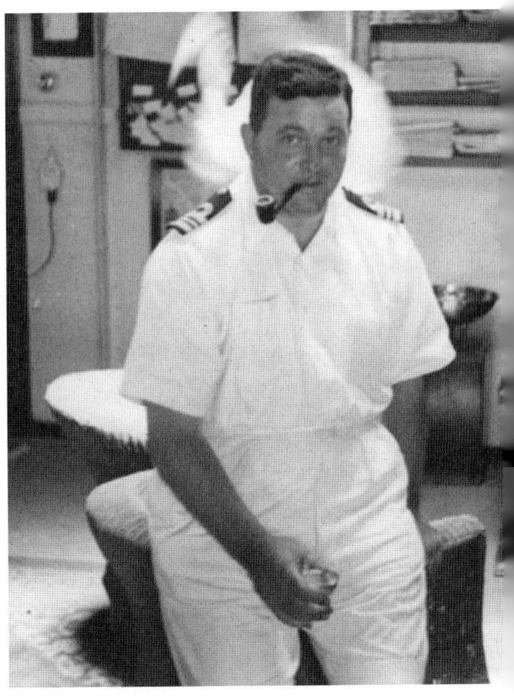

A beardless John Linton in his navy whites, holding a glass of wine and smoking a pipe.

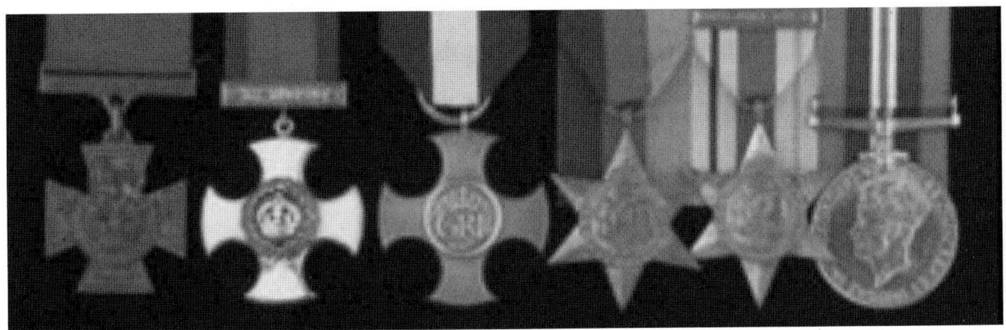

John Linton's medals from the Lord Ashcroft collection.

Blue plaque in the name of John Wallace Linton VC, in Newport.

The *Siestriere*, another POW vessel, was in convoy with the *Nino Bixio* when it was attacked by HMS *Turbulent* in August 1942.

The *Nino Bixio* was used by the Italians to transport Allied POWs from North Africa to the Italian mainland.

The *Nino Bixio* in harbour at an unknown port. Remarkably, the vessel survived the war and was still in use ten years later.

Wellington Harbour, New Zealand, when the *Nino Bixio* paid a visit for a wreath laying ceremony. Those pictured are New Zealand soldiers who survived the attack by *Turbulent*.

Crew member of HMS *Turbulent*, John Deller.

John Deller at dinner with his comrades.

John Deller's Royal Navy service card. Note the writing at the bottom: 'Missing and Presumed Killed - 23-3-43'.

No C/JX 200506

Rating H.O AB ST

NAME JOHN. H. DELLER.

Joined SM.'s

S.A.R.

N.S.A.R.

Recommended by

Ability

Prof. Exam

Educl. Exam

S M	Joined	REMARKS	S M	Joined	REMARKS
T.C.	31-3-41	Dolphin			
	2-5-41				
S/c	14.5.41.	Cyclops.			
Turbulent	10.9.41	Dolphin			
	3.1.42.	Medway			
S/c	18.1.43.	Talbot			
Turbulent		Medway			

Missing Presumed Killed

23.3.43

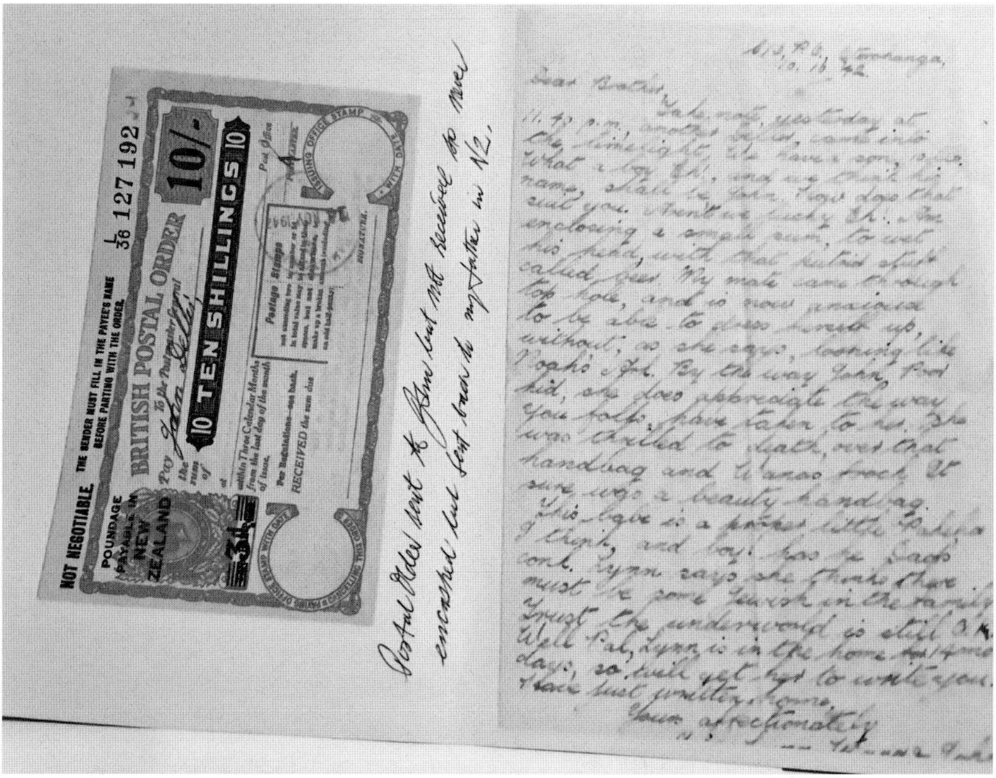

Letter and postal order sent to John Deller from his brother Jim. The letter is dated 10 October 1942, but it was never received.

Letter to John Deller dated 14 November 1942, but returned to sender. 'It is with the deepest regret that you are informed that the addressee is missing, presumed killed on Active Service.'

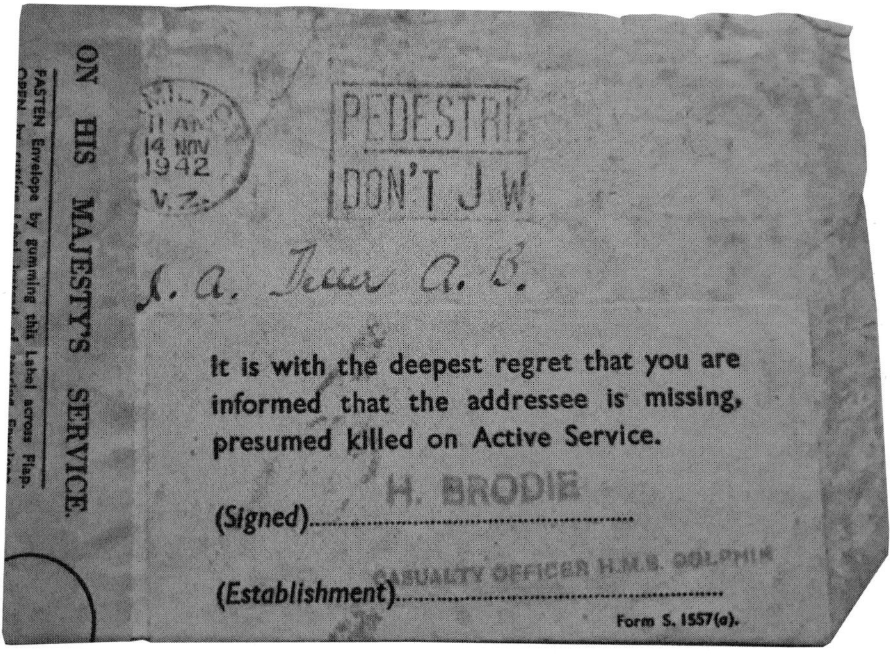
ON HIS MAJESTY'S SERVICE.

PEDESTRI
DON'T J W

14 NOV
1942

It is with the deepest regret that you are informed that the addressee is missing, presumed killed on Active Service.

(Signed)........ H. BRODIE

(Establishment)........ CASUALTY OFFICER H.M.S. DOLPHIN

Form S. 1557(a).

Ken Geenty, an Australian POW who survived the attack on the *Nino Bixio.*

A sketch by Ken Geenty showing that despite the experience of surviving the attack by *Turbulent*, and then later surviving life as a POW, he still had a sense of humour.

Australian POW Bill Rudd and New Zealand POW Charles James Watkins both survived the attack on the *Nino Bixio* by HMS *Turbulent*.

Peter Norton-Knight initially survived the attack on the *Nino Bixio*, but later died of diphtheria in an Italian hospital on 25 August 1942.

Peter's brother Gerald was also a POW on board the *Nino Bixio*.

The Norton-Knight brothers: Gerald (back row, far left), Peter (back row, third from left), and Maurice (front row, far left).

Submariners learning how to escape from a stricken submarine.

Whilst travelling in convoy, the Italian merchant vessel the *Anna Maria Gualdi* was attacked by HMS *Turbulent* on 29 May 1942, 75 nautical miles off the coast of Libya.

February 8 – Whilst in the region of Cape Gallo, Sicily, and much to the surprise of *Turbulent*'s Commander, John Linton, he came across a single and unescorted merchant vessel. Expecting to sink another enemy vessel, Linton was at somewhat of a loss to explain how the two torpedoes he had fired at a distance of 1,200 yards from their intended target, somehow managed to miss.

This scenario is actually quite staggering. An unescorted and unarmed enemy merchant ship, travelling without any escort (either another surface vessel or aircraft in the skies above), in essence made it a "sitting duck", and still *Turbulent* somehow managed to miss its target?

February 12 – Saw the end of *Turbulent*'s eleventh war patrol when she returned to Algiers to re-fuel, stock up on supplies, ammunition, and re-join the 8th Submarine Flotilla. The twelve days she was in Port also gave her officers and crew time to relax and recuperate.

February 24 – Saw *Turbulent* leave Algiers and begin her twelfth patrol in the area of the Mediterranean known as the Tyrrhenian Sea. The patrol also saw her sail through the waters north of Messina and the approaches to Naples.

March 1 – *Turbulent* came across the Italian merchant vessel *San Vincenzo*, a mile north-west of Paola. Initially she fired two torpedoes which both missed their intended target. Rising to the surface,

> *Turbulent* opened fire with her deck gun, eventually sinking the San Vincenzo.
>
> *Turbulent* was then ordered to make her way to the east coast of Corsica, with instructions to coast crawl to the south-east corner of Sardinia, reporting her arrival at this position. This *Turbulent* failed to do; at the time it was thought she had been mined off Maddalena.
>
> **March 11** – From Italian records it is evident that the *Turbulent* had attacked the Italian steamer, *Mafalda*, 8 miles off Bastia, Corsica, at about 1500 hours, missing her with two torpedoes. In consequence she was hunted by M.A.S.B.s [Motor Anti-Submarine Boats] and A/S [Anti-Submarine] craft sent out from Bastia.
>
> **March 12** – About 0900 a submarine was seen to break surface by one of the A/S craft and was attacked by gunfire and a pattern of eight depth charges, forcing her to submerge. She was considered to have been sunk.

HMS *Turbulent* was due to have returned to Algiers at the end of its patrol on 23 March 1943. The submarine was then due to return to the UK, and from there onwards to Philadelphia for a refit. Commander Linton and his crew never made it back to Algiers.

Nobody knows for certain exactly what happened to *Turbulent*. By way of example, the extract dated 12 March taken from *Turbulent's* own War Diary highlights this very point. It transpired that the attack as described against the *Turbulent* actually involved the French submarine, *Casablanca.*

The diary of George Svenson is particularly helpful as it is not *Turbulent's* official War Diary and is therefore more than likely to include information which might not have otherwise been recorded. It also explains that the last actual sighting and contact with *Turbulent* took place on 1 March 1943, when it attacked the Italian merchant vessel *San Vincenzo*, a mile north-west of Paola, and then received orders to make its way to the east coast of Corsica and report in on arrival. This *Turbulent* failed to do, meaning that its final resting place is potentially going to be even more difficult to locate. The distance between Paolo and Corsica is 180 kilometres, which is a long route to retrace if the remains of *Turbulent* are ever to be discovered.

Svenson's diary also provides an alternative impression of Linton compared with the one officially portrayed by the Admiralty, most notably when he refers to the commander as "that Captain Bligh", a clear reference to Lieutenant William Bligh, the man in charge of HMAV *Bounty* during the infamous mutiny of 1789, with some reports claiming the mutiny took place because of Bligh's tyrannical behaviour and abusive nature towards to his crew.

Possibly the most damming part of Svenson's diary, however, is his claim that he personally passed Linton the message informing him that the *Nino Bixio* was carrying allied POWs before he carried ordered Turbulent to carry out the attack.

CHAPTER SEVEN

Notes of Chief Petty Officer Sydney Charles Kay DSM

This chapter features the typed notes made by Chief Petty Officer Sydney Charles Kay, who served on HMS *Turbulent* from the time of its completion at Barrow, all the way through to Monday, 18 January 1943, when it arrived at Malta at the end of its tenth war patrol. Afterwards, Kay was admitted to St Andrews 18th Field hospital with rheumatic fever, where he remained until March 1943.

These notes were once again supplied by John Deller, the nephew of John Deller, the Able Seaman lost on board HMS *Turbulent* when it disappeared in March 1943.

By the beginning of the Second World War, Sydney Kay would have already been classed as an experienced submariner. He had enlisted in the Royal Navy way back in July 1921, and in November 1928, with seven years' service under his belt, he took the decision to volunteer for the submarine service. Before commencing his time with *Turbulent* in January 1941, he had already served on eight other submarines.

After returning to the UK to recover from his bout of rheumatic fever, he went on to serve on three other Royal Navy submarines, before finishing the war as an instructor on the training submarine, HMS *Dolphin*, in February 1945. He was awarded the Distinguished Service Medal in September 1942.

The notes begin with the following paragraph and proceed to detail his life on board.

> These recordings are rather brief and only mention attacks made by Torpedoes and Gunfire. Many other incidents represented by 'Scimitars' on the 'Jolly Roger' such as landing and picking up Commandos and Spies, I only recall briefly.
>
> I hope whoever reads this will enjoy doing so. Please do not deface or remove any of the pages.
>
> Signed S.C. Kay.
>
> **Saturday 3 January 1942** – Left Dunoon on completion of trials for the Mediterranean, doing a passage patrol en route for Gibraltar. No incidents.
>
> **Saturday 10 January** – Arrived Gibraltar.
>
> **Thursday 15 January** – Left Gibraltar for patrol in vicinity of Almeira Bay, Spain. No incidents.

During the Second World War, Gibraltar had a strongly defended harbour and served as an important location for British operations in both the Atlantic and the Mediterranean. Operation Torch, the Allied invasion of North Africa, was co-ordinated from Gibraltar, where American General, Dwight

D. Eisenhower, who was in overall command of the operation, had his headquarters.

HMS *Turbulent* would return to Gibraltar a week later, on 21 January, which was an unusually short period of time in which to conduct a patrol.

> **Monday 26 January** – Left Gibraltar for Malta.

> **Monday 2 February** – Arrived Malta after uneventful passage. Met Jan Hambly S/M P34, my old shipmate from my China days. HMS *Olympus*.

S/M P34 is a reference to HM Submarine *Ultimatum*, which had ended its seventh war patrol on 1 February 1942 at Malta, where it remained until 14 February before beginning its eighth war patrol. HMS *Ultimatum* and its crew, including Jan Hambly, survived the war.

HMS *Olympus*, an O-class submarine, was commissioned on 14 June 1930, and lost on 8 May 1942, when it struck a mine 7 miles off the coast of Malta. A total of eighty-nine crew and passengers were lost with only nine survivors, all of whom had to swim back to Malta.

> **Wednesday 4 February** – Left Malta for patrol off Suda Bay, Crete, whilst en route to Alexandria to join up with HMS *Medway.* There were two minor incidents on this patrol. We received our introduction to depth charges whilst off Suda Bay, but nothing to write about.

Being depth charged could not have been a nice experience. Not knowing after each subsequent explosion whether they might be killed must have been petrifying, regardless of how experienced the crew were. In the circumstances, one would have thought that Sydney would have had plenty to "write about".

> **Friday 13 February** – Arrived Alexandria and secured alongside HMS *Medway.*

HMS *Medway* (F25) was launched in July 1928 and completed in July the following year. The vessel was the Royal Navy's first ever purpose-built submarine depot ship, and was in Alexandria until 29 June 1942, before being ordered to leave by the Commander-in-Chief, Mediterranean Fleet, Vice-Admiral Henry Harwood, in the face of Rommel's advance in the region after the Battle of Gazala.

Medway which was part of a large convoy and carrying supplies and some 1,135 men, was en route to the new British base at Beirut, Lebanon, when it was attacked and sunk by German submarine *U-372* on 30 June. Thirty of the crew on board were killed.

Turbulent left Alexandria on 23 February. On board at the time was Lieutenant Commander Reginald Marbury Raymond of the United States Navy, acting in an official capacity as an observer. When not undertaking his liaison duties with the Royal Navy, Raymond served on board the USS *Scorpion*, a *Gato*-class submarine which had only been launched on 20 July 1942.

Monday, 23 February saw *Turbulent* begin its third war patrol. Three days later, on 26 February, it met a convoy off Suda Bay but was unable to attack. The convoy consisted of eleven German and Italian, merchant and military vessels, and in such situations, it was a finite decision for commanders such as John Linton to balance holding his position long enough to be able to affectively fire his torpedoes, against holding it too long and putting the safety of his submarine and crew in danger of being destroyed and killed. In return, the convoy attacked *Turbulent* by dropping depth charges.

> **Friday 27 February** – Attacked and sank an enemy kyack by gunfire. This kyack was carrying Italian soldiers. This was in the Doro Channel.

> **Monday 2 March** – Sank two enemy kyacks by gunfire at the entrance to Salonika Bay.

In *Turbulent's* official War Diary, what Sydney describes as "kyacks" are referred to as Greek caiques. The one sank on 27 February is stated to have been Pi 253/*Agios Charalambos.*

> **Tuesday 3 March** – Sank Nazi steam trawler by gunfire. This vessel was flying a Nazi ensign and had about 170 German soldiers aboard.

Turbulent's patrol reports and logbooks show a slightly different entry for the same day, 3 March:

> Sank a Greek caique with gunfire South of the Kassandra peninsula. The schooner, thought to be of 150 tons was seen to sink. This ship was the Greek caique *Kal 199 / Agios Dionyssios* (30 GRT). She was also transporting German soldiers. 16 were reported to have been killed.

Returning to Sydney Kay's notes:

> **Thursday 5 March** – Attacked and fired four torpedoes at enemy convoy consisting of two merchant ships and two destroyers. This was a night surface attack at 0249 hours. All torpedoes missed, because although *Turbulent* was not sighted, the enemy altered course to enter the pass through the Doro Channel just at the moment of firing. A second attack was not possible owing to very, very restrictive manoeuvring space and also one of the escorting destroyers was now heading in our direction.
>
> **Friday 6 March** – At 1054 hours sank enemy schooner by gunfire.
>
> **Tuesday 10 March** – Now in the Gulf of Athens; got sighted by enemy patrol vessels and were at the receiving end of fifty-four depth charges.

That most certainly would not have been a fun experience, in fact it must have been absolutely terrifying for the crew of *Turbulent.* If any one of the depth charges had caused the damage they were intended to, the submarine would have been sunk and all the crew on board at the time would have been lost.

Sydney's diary entries over the next few weeks are very brief and are best summarised as follows. In the period between 12 March and 10 April, *Turbulent* attacked a number of axis vessels, including the Greek caique *Agia Paraskevi,* which was attacked with gunfire at 0912 hours on Thursday,

12 March. The following day, at 0024 hours, the Greek caique *Kal 155/Anastassis* was sunk just west of Serifos in Greece. At 0700 hours on 17 March, having finished its third war patrol, *Turbulent* returned to Alexandria, having accounted for 1,500 tons worth of enemy vessels, all by gunfire.

Turbulent began its fourth war patrol on Monday, 30 March, leaving Alexandria at 1800 hours at what was the start of a 24-day period at sea. Its first success took place on Tuesday, 7 April when it attacked and sank a 1,500-ton steam ship, once again by gunfire, which was carrying motor cars and trucks. The vessel in question is believed to have been the Italian merchant ship the *Rosa M.* On Thursday, 9 April *Turbulent* attacked an unknown enemy merchant vessel, but both the torpedoes fired missed their target, and before *Turbulent* could re-manoeuvre into position to fire again, it was deterred from doing so by escorting vessels. On Friday, 10 April *Turbulent* fired four torpedoes at an enemy vessel, but somewhat remarkably, all four missed and the opportunity was gone.

On Sunday, 12 April *Turbulent* spotted an Italian submarine on the surface off Fiume, Italy, but as it prepared to attack, the Italian submarine dived and escaped. Sydney believed that it was a training vessel, although why he thought that is unclear.

On Monday, 13 April, *Turbulent* fired two torpedoes at a 2,000-ton steam ship, but both ran under the vessel.

The Royal Navy had an on-going problem with torpedoes missing their targets throughout the war. This happened for a number of reasons. Some were the result of human error; some were down to enemy ships manoeuvring out of the way; whilst other misses took place because of incorrect depth settings on the torpedoes or because of malfunctions. Most had an effective range of no more than 5,000 yards. Nevertheless, reading through Sydney's memories of his time on board *Turbulent*, it is quite shocking that so many of the torpedoes failed to hit their targets, which could not have been good for the crews' morale.

> **Tuesday 14 April** – Attacked enemy schooner by gunfire but shore battery opened fire at us and we had to dive.
>
> **Thursday 16 April** – Attacked and fired two torpedoes at a 6,000 ton fully laden supply vessel [the *Della*] off Monopoli, near Brindisi. Both torpedoes hit and vessel sank in three minutes. This was a very satisfactory and cheerful end to what had been a very disappointing patrol. It was verified later that although the depth settings on the first eight torpedoes which missed had been set to 6 feet, they ran under the targets because they were in ballast. We now decided to leave the Adriatic and head back to Alexandria, patrolling en route.
>
> **Saturday 18 April** – 2200 we received a signal to intercept a convoy. We made our way at full speed on the surface but we had no luck.
>
> **Tuesday 20 April** – Arrived back at Alexandria. Tonnage sunk this patrol: 6,000 tons by torpedo, 1,500 tons by gunfire. Total tonnage to date: 9,000 tons.

Alexandria was a major British naval base for submarines and surface vessels, and had first opened in 1916. In April 1942 it was under the command of Rear Admiral George Hector

Cresswell. There was also a shore establishment that was situated at Ras el-Tin Point.

Monday 11 May – Left Alexandria for Benghazi patrol.

Thursday 14 May – Sank two large enemy schooners (each 500 tons) by gunfire. They were full of ammunition.

Sunday 17 May – Surfaced and sighted enemy convoy.

Monday 18 May – Convoy was shadowed until 0300 hours then the attack commenced. Two torpedoes were fired at one 4,000-ton ship which was hit and sunk. A third torpedo was fired at a second ship, but this missed because the escort destroyers had sighted us and was coming at us at full speed. We dived to 90 feet to wait for the depth charges. However, after only dropping five depth charges, the escort tailed off to accompany the second ship which had had a lucky escape from us and was making off at full speed.

Tuesday 26 May – We sighted a convoy and were proceeding to attack when we were sighted by aircraft and escorting vessels. We were forced down and unable to attack. Fortunately, only nineteen depth charges were dropped by one escorting vessel whilst the convoy made a getaway.

Friday 29 May – 0330. Began a surface attack on four large supply ships. When in position we dived to periscope depth and commenced the attack. Four torpedoes were fired and three hits were registered.

It is worth dwelling on this attack for a few moments to explain a little more in detail of what happened. The first torpedo hit and sank a 6,000 ton supply ship. The second torpedo hit and sank a 4,000 ton supply ship. By this time one of the escorting destroyers had got a bearing on our position and was coming at us at full speed. However, our captain was determined to get another supply ship before going deep. No. 3 torpedo was fired and five seconds later No. 4. Then just as we were going to go deep, the thunderous crash of the destroyer's propellers was distinctively heard, followed by a very large explosion. We in the sub naturally thought, "here we go, it's our turn now". Stand by for the ash cans. But oh dear no, not yet. Surprise, surprise, the third torpedo when fired had a gyro failure causing it to run round in a circle after it left the torpedo tube, and by a most fortunate piece of luck for us, whilst the torpedo was making its circle it hit the destroyer making the attack on us, [striking] perfectly up the stern between the propellers just as it had passed over us. This was no flick of imagination on our part but was verified by aerial photographs taken by our spotter planes which were overhead during the action. In fact, this hit was not claimed or known to us until after we returned off patrol to Alexandria and the photo was shown.

I don't know where the fourth torpedo ended up amongst all the noise. Probably on the bottom of the ocean. But all we received from the other escorts whilst all this was going on were twenty-three depth charges.

The Italian navy did its utmost to help keep a constant supply of men, equipment, ammunition, and food for Italian and German forces fighting in North Africa, but they were hampered in their attempts not only by Royal Navy submarines, but large numbers of mines which had been laid by the British between Sicily and Tunis.

> **Tuesday 2 June** – We are now on our way back to Alexandria and just off Tobruk on the surface proceeding on one engine and charging batteries on the other. We had been dived all day and the batteries were low, due to having been down for so long. This time of the year there was long daylight. Suddenly one of the look-outs reported 'U-boat.' Diving stations was ordered and six torpedoes were brought to the ready. Four torpedoes were fired but missed, although four explosions were heard and it was presumed there had been a second U-boat dived in the vicinity and by good luck we had hit it. We did not claim a kill for this. However, the first 'U-boat' was still on the surface and a further two torpedoes were fired, and both scored hits. Exit one 'U-boat'. We now dived and proceeded along submerged for a couple of hours after which we surfaced and steamed at full speed to get clear of the area. This 'U-boat' we claimed was a small one of about 500 tons.
>
> **Thursday 4 June** – We arrived back in Alexandria. We were met in the 'Sanctuary' by Commander H.C. Browne, Staff Officer Operations, and it was then that we were informed about our sinking of the destroyer during the attack on the convoy on 29 May.

He noticed the destroyer was missing from our Jolly Roger. It was then he informed us of our success and later showed us aerial photos taken by our aircraft.

Commander Hector Christopher Browne had previously been in command of the Royal Navy submarine HMS *Regent,* with whom he had served for the first couple of years of the war.

Before moving to his next entry, Kay provided the figures for their latest patrol:

Tonnage sunk this patrol:

Two schooners by gunfire, 500 tons.

Two 4,000-ton supply ships, 8,000 tons.

One 6,000-ton supply ship, 6,000 tons.

One destroyer, 1,600 tons.

One U-boat, 500 tons.

Total for this patrol: 16,600 tons. Total tonnage to date: 25,600 tons.

Monday 5 June – Left Alexandria again for patrol off Benghazi.

Monday 22 June – Attacked one merchant ship and one destroyer off Benghazi. First two torpedoes missed. The destroyer came on to attack us but after

> only dropping seven depth charges went off at full speed, together with the merchant ship.

This was an example of the difficult decisions that convoy escorts had to face when seeing off an attacking enemy vessel. They would do their best to attack and destroy it, but the longer they were engaged in such activities, the longer the convoy they were there to defend was in danger of potentially being attacked by other submarines in the area.

> **Tuesday 23 June** – Intercepted convoy bound for Benghazi whose position we had received from spotter aircraft. Before we could carry out an attack, we were spotted by aircraft which bombed us, followed later by depth charges from escort vessels. We surfaced when all was quiet, and during the night, after shadowing the convoy, we prepared to attack again.

> **Wednesday 24 June** – Attacked the above convoy again, this time firing two torpedoes and hitting a 2,000-ton supply ship with both torpedoes. She sank very quickly but we could not watch this because we were spotted by aircraft and escort vessels. Again, we received a shower of bombs and depth charges. Whilst this was going on we laid on the bottom in 60 feet of water. This, under normal conditions, would have been fatal, but due to it being a sandy bottom the exploding bombs and depth charges churned up the sand so much it obscured us from the aircraft and also made it difficult for the escort vessels to locate us on their hydrophones or asdics [sonar].

> **Tuesday 30 June** – This was a sad day for us for we received the signal that HMS *Medway* (our mother ship), has been sunk by a 'U-boat' whilst on passage from Alexandria to Haifa. Rommel was advancing so rapidly towards Cairo it had been decided to evacuate Alexandria. HM Destroyers *Zulu* and *Hero* picked up all survivors. We, and all the subs operating from Alexandria, were now without a base. However, a base for us was found at Beirut, Lebanon.

HMS *Medway* (F25), a submarine tender under the command of Captain Philip Ruck-Keene CBE RN, was sunk by torpedoes fired by the German submarine *U-372* under the command of Korvettenkapitan Heinz-Joachim Neumann. Out of a crew of 1,135, 1,105 were saved, along with more than half of the 90 torpedoes that were on board. The submarine had been well-protected on its journey from Alexandria, with an escort of eight vessels including seven destroyers. Despite this, HMS *Medway* was unable to fulfil its journey.

U-372 was sunk on 4 August 1942, south-west of the Israeli city of Haifa, by a combination of depth charges and aerial bombing. The attack was carried out by four destroyers of the British Royal Navy, HMS *Croome*, HMS *Sikh,* HMS *Tetcott*, and HMS *Zulu.* An RAF Wellington bomber aircraft also took part in the attack. All members of the German submarine crew survived and became prisoners of war.

Four days after HMS *Medway* was sunk, Sydney Kay continued his diary entries.

> **Saturday 4 July** – Intercepted and commenced to get into position to make an attack on a convoy of three large supply ships which must have been

very valuable because they had an escort of eight destroyers. Unfortunately, before we could even start the attack, we were spotted and compelled to go deep whilst the depth charges were being dropped. Needless to say, when all was quiet enough for us to take a look around at periscope depth and then surface, there wasn't a sign of anything on the water.

Wednesday 15 July – We arrived at Beirut, Lebanon, and secured alongside an Italian submarine which had been captured and brought in to harbour the day before by HM Corvette K14. A very interesting thing to record about this:- After being brought into harbour, the enemy (British) mounted guard and searched throughout to see there were no demolition charges set to go off. They came loaded with talcum powder, scents, soap, cigarettes and miscellaneous other goods which had been taken from the crew's lockers. It caused quite a laugh.

This was the end of *Turbulent's* sixth war patrol. Returning to port must have been such a relief to the men who served on submarines, because no matter how much they enjoyed being a submariner, the feelings they must have experienced when they arrived safely back to their home port can only be guessed at. Being on board for such a long period of time, with the added stress of being at war, knowing that at any moment they might die a horrible death, must have been horrendous. To have lived and worked in such a cramped, humid and smelly environment for the better part of a month, would not have been for the feint hearted.

On 18 July, Kay reports that Georges Albert Julien Catroux, a five-star General in the French Army, visited *Turbulent*. In 1915 he had been captured by the Germans and spent the rest of the war as a prisoner, during which time he became acquainted with another French soldier, Captain Charles de Gaulle.

In July 1940, he joined de Gaulle in London as part of the French government in exile. He became a member of Charles de Gaulle's first government, which lasted between 9 September 1944 to 21 October 1945, having been appointed as the Minister for North Africa. Soon afterward he was appointed ambassador to the USSR, a position he held until 1948.

On Monday, 20 July *Turbulent* received a visit in Beirut from General Edward Spears, in his capacity as the Minister to Syria and Lebanon, a position he had held since January 1942. In his diary entry, Sydney Kay had incorrectly spelt his name as Spiers.

> **Wednesday 22 July** – Half of *Turbulent*'s crew went up to the mountains to the Hotel Windsor at Aley for five days. This was being used as a rest camp for submarine crews. Coxswain George Wilks was in charge of the first half which went on 16 July. I was in charge of the second party which went later.

The Windsor Hotel was officially opened in 1924 and, prior to the outbreak of the Second World War, attracted guests from all over the world with its opulence and style. Its rooftop bar and restaurant offered astonishing views down into heart of Beirut and the sea beyond, making it an ideal location to rest and recuperate in between war patrols.

The Commonwealth War Graves Commission records that George Harold Wilks died on 23 March 1943, the date *Turbulent* was due to have returned from patrol. He has no known grave and is commemorated on the Chatham Naval Memorial. He was a holder of the Distinguished Service Order.

After another two weeks in Beirut, *Turbulent* set sail for its seventh war patrol, this time in the Ionian Sea, on Wednesday, 5 August.

> **Monday 16 August** – In position 25 miles off Navarin, we attacked a convoy of two 8,000-ton merchant ships with three destroyers as escort. A salvo of four torpedoes was fired. A hit was scored on one of the ships by the first torpedo. The second torpedo had a gyro failure and missed. Both the third and fourth torpedoes hit the second ship. Both these ships sank in very quick time. No. 2 torpedo which had the gyro failure gave us a very uncomfortable feeling because it passed over us three times whilst circling round and eventually going to the bottom and exploding. The three escort destroyers must have either seen or detected the gyro failure torpedo on their hydrophones and maybe thought it was a secret weapon because they gave us a wide berth and eventually steamed away without dropping even one depth charge.

Although this entry is dated Monday, 16 August, it quite clearly describes the attack on the *Nino Bixio*, which took place in mid-afternoon on Tuesday, 17 August, as is recorded in *Turbulent's* patrol reports and logbooks. These list the attack as taking place 12 nautical miles south-west of Navarino, and not 25 miles as stated by Sydney Kay. He also does not mention the *Nino Bixio* by name, but in fairness, he also fails to name any of the other vessels *Turbulent* attacked.

Tuesday 1 September – Arrived back in Beirut. Tonnage this patrol, 16,000. Total tonnage to date, 43,600.

Whilst we were on this last patrol the survivors of HMS *Medway* arrived at Beirut and took over an old French army barracks, five miles out in the desert from Beirut. Apparently this place was in a very dirty and deplorable state, but after much hard work it was brought up to Royal Naval Standards. It was named HMS *Medway II.* It was used by ex-Medway crew as living accommodation and administration offices. The crews of other submarines also stayed there having returned to Beirut for their short break between patrols, but still returned to their respective submarines each day to work. All the workshops, (Engineers, Torpedoes, etc), were situated in various buildings down at the harbour, close to where the submarines were berthed.

Monday 14 September – Turbulent left Beirut for Port Said, to go on the floating dock for the bottom to be scrapped. We also had our fresh water tanks cleansed and inspected.

Wednesday 16 September – Arrived Port Said and went on floating dock. During our stay in Port Said the non-duty watches were accommodated in the Italian opera house, for eating and sleeping. The duty watch each day stayed in the submarine. This was a kind of easy break before going out on patrol.

Sunday 20 September – Commander John W. Linton DSC RN informed us he had been informed by signal that he had been awarded the DSC. Also that Lieutenant R.B. Foster RN (our 1st Lieutenant) and Lieutenant P.F.N Parker RN (Engineer Lieutenant) had been awarded the DSC. The DSM had been awarded to the following ratings: Chief Petty Officer S.C. Kay, D/J 97405, (whose notes these are) Chief Petty Officer/ Telegraphist W.K. Hadley P/J 107992, Chief Petty Officer/ Coxswain G.H. Wilks C/JX 125656, Engine Room Artificer 1st Class P.E. King D/MX 50475, Electrical Artificer 1st Class F.C. Morris C/M 38173, Stoker/Petty Officer W.F. Sharp D/K 66108, Leading Seaman R.R.I. Feasy C/ JX 141258, Gun Layer/Acting Leading Telegraphist W. Richardson P/JX 154518. [The citation in the *London Gazette* for these awards was: "For courage and skill in successful submarine patrols on HMS *Turbulent*."]

Sydney Kay's notes show that *Turbulent* undocked on Monday, 21 September, although surprisingly this is not recorded in the official log.

On 22 September it left Port Said at 1830 for patrol off Tobruk, Derna and Benghazi. This was the beginning of its eighth war patrol. Nearly all its crew had remained the same throughout these patrols, which, morale wise, would have been of great assistance to the smooth running and level of discipline on board.

Wednesday 30 September – Received signal of a convoy off Tobruk. We surfaced and proceeded at 16 knots to intercept.

Thursday 1 October – Sighted convoy at 0300. It was approximately 6 miles away and was being attacked by aircraft. Convoy consisted of one 10,000 tanker and two destroyers. We dived at 0650 hours to make our attack. The attack was not carried out due to the convoy and escort taking so much evasive action in altering course to avoid the air attack. We were unable to get into position to attack.

Tuesday 6 October – Sighted and attacked a convoy consisting of one merchant ship and four destroyers north of Benghazi. We fired three torpedoes but all missed due to convoy altering course. Also escort vessels picked us up on their hydrophones and carried out prolonged depth-charging. When it was quiet enough to come up to periscope depth there was nothing in sight.

Wednesday 7 October – At 0630 hours we sighted a convoy of one merchant ship and four destroyers (probably the one we had attacked the day before). The weather conditions were very bad this particular day. Low cloud, poor visibility and frequent heavy rainstorms. We manoeuvred to get in a favourable attacking position, but before the attack could be carried out a very heavy rainstorm opened up. It was so heavy and lasted so long that when eventually visibility cleared, there was nothing in sight.

Thursday 8 October – 0130 hours sighted and attacked one 1,000 ton tanker. Fired two torpedoes. Got one hit which sank the tanker, second torpedo missed.

Wednesday 14 October – Arrived back in Beirut 0600 hours. Tonnage sunk this patrol 1,000. Total tonnage to date 44,600.

This marked the end of *Turbulent's* eighth war patrol, but it was back out again a week later for its ninth patrol, sailing to Malta on 28 October and arriving on 4 November at 1030 hours.

Thursday 5 November – 0400 hours left Malta to commence patrol off Sardinia. The whole of the sea area between Malta and Sicily was very heavily mined. It was commonly known as, and referred to as, 'Bomb Alley'. (Surface ships going to Malta from the west and again when leaving to sail back to the west, generally Gibraltar, had the double hazard to contend with, i.e., bombs from enemy aircraft and the very extensive minefields). Submarines having to pass through this minefield invariably dived deep and felt their way by using their Asdics [sonar]. We passed through at 60 feet.

Friday 6 November – We arrived at our first patrol area off Cagliari, Sardinia.

Saturday 7 November – 0030 hours night alarm sounded. Enemy A/S schooner heard approaching. Tried to get in favourable position to attack by gun fire but visibility was bad. 0200 night alarm again sounded. It was the same A/S schooner but this time no attempt to attack was made. It was thought if we had done so, the bigger planes we were hoping for might be scared off.

Sunday 8 November – We received the joyful news that the United States Army had landed at Oran and Algiers.

This was a reference to the Allied amphibious landings in North Africa, which had taken place that day at Algiers and Oran, as well as Casablanca, with the main resistance being met at the latter two locations. Nevertheless, the element of surprise achieved by the Americans during the landings greatly reduced the number of casualties they incurred, but two days later the Americans at Oran had still made little headway as they found themselves up against some stiff resistance from the French Vichy regime.

Wednesday 11 November – Sighted and attacked large armed merchant cruiser of 4,000 tons on course to enter Cagliari. This vessel was flying a large Nazi ensign. Two torpedoes were fired. The first one unfortunately ran deep and missed, but the second one made a hit on the stern. There was a terrific explosion, so much so that the whole of the aft gun's crew were blown into the sea. The ship sank in a matter of minutes. It was announced by the Italians later that this vessel was a submarine supply ship and it may have been of more tonnage than we claimed.

Friday 13 November – Received signal of three Italian battleships and eleven destroyers and ordered to proceed at full speed to intercept.

Saturday 14 November – In position given but did not sight the Italian battleships or destroyers. Proceeding to the Gulf of Naples, our new patrol area.

Interestingly, there is no mention in *Turbulent*'s official log book or patrol reports in relation to Sydney's entries for 13 and 14 November.

Sunday 15 November – Carried out a night surface attack on enemy tanker and one destroyer escort. Fired four torpedoes but all missed. Weather conditions at the time were very bad indeed.

Tuesday 17 November – Received our recall signal to leave the area on Wednesday 18th.

Wednesday 18 November – 1800 hours left the area to proceed back to Malta.

Thursday 19 November – Weather conditions extremely bad, remained at 80 feet all day.

Friday 20 November – Entered minefield (bomb alley) and passed through at 80 feet.

Saturday 21 November – 1500 hours, arrived Malta and tied up at HMS *Talbot* S/M berth.

Sunday 22 November – 0800 hours proceeded to torpedo depot to disembark torpedoes for use of submarines based at Malta. 1530 hours, left Malta to proceed back to Beirut, carrying out patrol in Gulf of Sirte en route.

Monday 23 November – On surface all day. Nothing sighted.

Tuesday 24 November – 0600 hours, dived off the town of Sirte. No shipping targets sighted. In the afternoon it was observed there were a large number of German tanks and miscellaneous mechanised units of Rommel's retreating Afrika Corps entering the town and parking in a large open space off the sea front (probably the town square). All this activity was kept under observation, and when the town square was full of these mechanised units, we surfaced and opened fire with our 4-inch gun. At very short range considerable havoc was caused during the fifteen minutes the gun action lasted. We then withdrew and dived because by this time the enemy had overcome their surprise and were firing at us. There were enemy ships in the vicinity, but we remained dived until nightfall when we surfaced to charge batteries and do a surface patrol.

What is strange here is that despite there being hundreds of newspaper articles commenting on Rommel's retreat across North Africa, there are no reports mentioning a number of his vehicles being attacked from the sea by a British submarine whilst in Sirte. One explanation for the omission as to why the German authorities made no official comment about the attack might have been because by doing so, not only did they risk confirming the exact position of their forces to the Allies, but they might also negatively affect the morale of their own men.

> **Wednesday 25 November** – At daybreak we dived to continue our patrol. Shortly after diving we hit a submerged wreck. This particular area was littered with wrecks so it wasn't much of a surprise to hit one. However, no damage was sustained and another uneventful day passed.

Turbulent was extremely fortunate that it did not sustain more serious, or even catastrophic damage. It was also rather fortunate that it was coming to the end of its patrol and that on arrival back at its new base in Beirut, it was possible to conduct an expedient and thorough examination of the submarine. It is also very unusual for such an occurrence to be deemed unnecessary to record in the *Turbulent's* official log book. The only logical conclusion that can be drawn is that the British authorities did not want to risk Germany discovering what had happened. In addition to this, if the matter had been officially recorded there would have no doubt been a formal enquiry, which would certainly have come to the attention of the Germans and would not have reflected well on Linton's reputation.

Turbulent arrived back in Beirut on 2 December, having completed its ninth war patrol. By this time, the crew would undoubtedly have been in need of a much needed and well-deserved break, and Sydney's four-day leave began the next day.

At the time, Beirut was considered by many to be the Paris of the Middle East, not just because of its bars, clubs and nightlife, but also because of its numerous art galleries, museums and places of historical interest.

Sydney spent some of his leave at the sergeant's mess, where mealtimes had somewhat of a formal feeling to them. Although located within the confines of the Royal Engineers Barracks, it was far from being just an ordinary working man's style canteen. There were no queues, with men being allocated a table that had already been laid with cutlery set out, and a bottle of wine placed carefully in the middle. After selecting their meal from a menu, they were served by a waiter.

The choice of wine was limited and was usually of a local blend of grape. Although cheap, it was what might be described as an acquired taste and was definitely not to everybody's liking, although it was preferable to the local tap water, which they were not advised to drink.

Friday 4 December – I took Richie and Wally (two sergeant friends) out to HMS *Medway II* where a social evening was being held in the Chief and Petty Officers' canteen.

Saturday 5 December – Returned with Richie and Wally to sergeants' mess, Beirut.

Sunday 6 December – I had the loan of an army motorcycle and went up to Aley in the mountains for the day to see some of the lads at the submarine rest camp.

Monday 7 December – Returned to duty from general leave.

Friday 18 December – 1800 hours, *Turbulent* left Beirut for Malta, with mails and every imaginable food required to make Christmas fare. (Nuts, cake, fruit, turkeys, new potatoes, cauliflowers and cabbage, you name it, we had it on board). All this for the submarine crews of the 10th Flotilla HMS *Talbot*, Malta.

This marked the beginning of *Turbulent*'s tenth war patrol, as they set out into the Mediterranean.

Saturday 19 December – Proceeded all day on surface but had to crash dive twice to avoid enemy aircraft.

Sunday 20 December – Again proceeded all day on the surface. No incidents.

Tuesday 22nd December – Dived during the forenoon's practice, gun action was carried out at noon. We have dived again until nightfall.

Wednesday 23 December – 1030 hours, arrived Malta and tied up alongside HMS Talbot to disembark all the Christmas food we had brought. After disembarking food, *Turbulent* laid off and moored out in the creek between two buoys. (This was the usual safety measure in case of enemy air-raids).

HMS Talbot was the shore base for Royal Navy submarines at Malta. The Admiralty had identified Malta as the ideal location for a submarine base even before the outbreak of the Second World War, although the base did not become operational until February 1941. It ensured that Italian forces fighting against the British in North Africa were not so easily supplied with men, ammunition, food and equipment.

HMS Talbot, which was located at Manoel Island in Marsamxett Harbour, did not have an easy existence. Besides being home to the 10th Submarine Flotilla, the base also comprised maintenance workshops and accommodation for the submariners and the shore-based skilled naval workers who carried out all the required repairs on the submarines.

Throughout the second half of 1940 in particular, the island of Malta was bombed extensively by the German Luftwaffe, forcing any Royal Navy submarines that were not out on patrol to take refuge on the harbour's seabed. Besides the obvious dangers which came with German bombing raids, the clear blue waters of the Mediterranean presented, some would say, an even bigger and ever-present danger to Royal Navy submarines, especially for the older and larger ones. Indeed, more were located by German aircraft flying overhead than those pinged on the sonar of a U-boat or surface vessel.

Thursday 24 December – Christmas Eve. As we were staying in Malta for Christmas, we took the opportunity of meeting as many of our friends in the Malta subs as we could.

Friday 25 December – Christmas Day. As *Turbulent* was still moored off in the creek, we had to go ashore to wish our 10th S/M flotilla friends a Happy Christmas, and of course there were many visitors to the *Turbulent* expressing their good wishes. The Malta submarine crews had their Christmas dinners in the base messes, but we in *Turbulent* had ours in

> the boat, and a real festive meal it was, thoroughly enjoyed by all of us.

Despite the fact that conditions inside *Turbulent* would have been extremely cramped for all concerned, at least they were in a position to enjoy the comparative calm waters that came with being in the harbour at Malta, rather than out at sea on patrol.

> **Saturday 26 December** – 1300 hours, sailed from Malta for patrol off Sardinia and Naples via the south channel Pantalaria.

> **Sunday 27 December** – Dived all day. After surfacing at nightfall, we had to crash dive due to one of our Wellington aircraft dropping marker flares on us in mistake for an enemy submarine.

Identification of vessels by either side was problematic. A sonar ping would identify the presence of another submarine in the immediate area, but what it could not show was whose side it was on. The identification of an enemy submarine on the surface was not any easier to achieve, unless of course the said vessel was displaying its ensign.

> **Monday 28 December** – Dived all day and arrived off Cagliari at 2200 hours.

> **Tuesday 29 December** – 1645 hours, attacked a fully loaded supply ship of 4,500 tons. Fired two torpedoes. First one missed but second one hit and ship sank very quickly. In reply to this Christmas box from

us to the Nazis, we only received six depth charges. These were dropped by the same small A/S vessel we had sighted in this position on our previous patrol.

On 29 December *Turbulent* actually attacked and sank two vessels, not one, as Sydney's report suggests. One of the two was the unnamed merchant vessel he mentioned, a 4,500-ton supply ship, which was struck by one torpedo, and the other was, according to *Turbulent's* log, the 5,290-ton Italian merchant vessel, the *Marte.* How many torpedoes it was struck by is unclear, but the location of the vessel's sinking is calculated as being 2 miles east of Cape Ferrato, Sardinia.

Wednesday 30 December – Changed our patrol to N E corner of Sardinia.

Thursday 31 December – Dived all day en route to patrol area off Naples. No incidents.

Friday 1 January 1943 – During the afternoon whilst on watch in the torpedo compartment, I was taken ill with acute rheumatism which later developed into rheumatic fever. I was wrapped in blankets and made as comfortable as possible on a shipside locker come bunk in the Chief and PO's mess. Within a few hours my ankles and knees were terribly swollen and all my joints were almost rigid. There was nothing that could be done to help matters. The only things in the medicine chest applicable to my sickness was an 8-ounce bottle of linament [sic], which was applied very sparingly once a day when the pain was most severe. There was also a bottle of Lover [liver]

> tablets. I had one of these each day when the pain was really severe.
>
> Everybody in the boat was extremely good. Commander Linton came at least once a day to see me. Petty Officer Jock Hogg, our 2nd coxswain, was marvellous. It was he who applied the linament [sic] and gave me the liver tablets. Our coxswain CPO George Wilks, who would normally have done all these things, was himself laid up with quinsy. All this and fourteen more days more to carry on patrol before returning to Malta.

Quinsy, or Peritonsillar abscess as it is also known, presents itself as a whitish, swollen blister or boil at the back of the throat. There are numerous symptoms, including a sore throat, swelling of the neck and face, difficulty in swallowing, fever and chills, as well as swollen lymph glands. One of the main causes can be untreated tonsillitis, but it can also occur from other ailments such as tooth infections or even smoking, and rarely occurs without an individual having previously had some kind of infection.

The medical officer on board HMS *Turbulent* was certainly good at his job, especially being able to diagnose George Wilks whilst under the stressful conditions of being on a war patrol.

> **Monday 11 January** – We were dived close inshore off Cape Bonifacio when at 0600 hours a medium supply ship of 2,500 tons was sighted making for the harbour. Two torpedo tubes were brought to the ready and when we were in a suitable firing position, two torpedoes were fired. Unfortunately,

> both missed because although we had not been sighted, the ship altered course. We then surfaced and opened fire with our 4-inch gun. A number of hits were made so much so it was observed that one of the ship's lifeboats had been lowered full of men, and it appeared as if the ship was being abandoned. Another torpedo was fired but this missed due to the ship making another alteration of course. We again opened fire with the gun making numerous hits, and on trying to take evasive action, the ship this time ran aground. By this time we had been sighted by shore batteries and they didn't waste any time opening fire. We didn't like leaving our target because she was only aground on a sandy shore and might later have been salvaged. We dived again and a fourth torpedo was fired, this made a direct hit and blew the ship to pieces. As all this had been happening so close to shore, and as we had made our presence very obvious, it was decided to remain dived and leave the area, before any surface craft were sent to search for us.

Turbulent's log records another incident for the same day which saw it surface and open fire with its 4-inch gun on the railway station at San Lucido. Only relatively minor damage was caused, especially taking into account the number of rounds that were fired. The attack came to an end when shore batteries returned fire, forcing *Turbulent* to withdraw and dive.

> **Tuesday 12 January** – We are now in a new position along the coast hoping as before that we might sight some trains and give our gun's crew a different kind

> of target. We were lucky because towards mid-day an electric train was observed coming along the coast where it was very open. We surfaced and opened fire. The marksmanship of our gun's crew was so good by now that a hit was made by the first shell fired. Only a few more shells were fired to completely destroy the train and do much carnage to the railway track. We dived again and proceeded out to sea in case of enemy action. One flying boat was observed but it apparently didn't see us. This proved to be our last incident on this transport.
>
> **Monday 18 January** – Arrived back in Malta. Tonnage sunk this patrol 2,500 plus one electric train. Total tonnage to date 51,100.
>
> At 1500 hours the same day I was transferred to St Andrews 18th Field Hospital where I remained for some weeks to slowly recover from my rheumatic fever.

St Andrews had also been a military hospital during the First World War, when it was a major location for the treatment of wounded soldiers from the Gallipoli campaign of April 1915. It was made up of nine buildings, each of which were able to accommodate 144 beds. Eight of the buildings were turned in to surgical wards, with the ninth being a medical ward. Two of the barracks' other buildings were used as a dispensary and an isolation ward. Medical staff from the Royal Army Medical Corps treated the wounded, with their accommodation being in the form of tents in the grounds of the barracks.

Sydney's diary entry for 18 January continues:

> My captain, Commander John W. Linton DSC, came up to the hospital to see me later. As I would not be fit enough to re-join the crew before *Turbulent* left on her next patrol, Commander Linton informed me he had promoted Leading Seaman Walker LTO, to Petty Officer and was taking him in my place as TGR. His parting words to me were; "Get well and be waiting for us when we get home. We will have a beer to celebrate."
>
> That for me was the end of a happy commission with a captain I was pleased to serve under, together with a crew of splendid shipmates. When *Turbulent* left Malta on her next patrol I believe she was again lucky in sinking a large supply ship of 7,000 tons. On completion of this patrol, she went to Algiers to be under the orders S/M depot ship HMS *Maidstone.* It was from Algiers that Turbulent went on her next patrol and from which she never returned.

The following is an extract from Rear Admiral G.W.G. Simpson's Professional Autobiography, 'Periscope View': "HM Submarine *Turbulent* sunk by escort vessels after making an attack on steamer Mafaldo off Bastia, Corsica, having fired two torpedoes which missed, March 1943."

The book by Rear Admiral Simpson was about the exploits of the Royal Navy's 10th Submarine Flotilla, who were based at Malta between 1941 and 1943, and which included HM Submarine *Turbulent.*

When I was well enough to leave hospital, I was invalided home and came home by sea (surface craft) via Port Said and South Africa and after ninety-eight days en route arrived at Liverpool on the Tuesday after Whitsun, June 1943.

It was whilst in a transit camp at Pietermaritsburg, South Africa that I read in the morning newspaper of the presumed loss of HMS *Turbulent.* When I eventually arrived at Fort Blockhouse, HMS *Dolphin*, at noon on the Wednesday, the day after arriving at Liverpool, I walked into the Chief Petty Officer's Mess and Chief Joiner Bob Savage was issuing the rum. When he saw me he seemed struck dumb, then said, and I quote, "Trapper, you are dead". (Trapper was a nom de plume given to me many years previously when serving in a submarine in China.) I told him he was talking rubbish, but he told me that only the day before when I was actually arriving at Liverpool, he had put up in the 'Memorial Chapel' the Memorial Tablet to the *Turbulent* and that my name was on it.

Whilst we were talking, I received a message I was wanted over at the Chaplain's office. I went over and was handed some letters and magazines from some of *Turbulent*'s mail. Whilst receiving them the chaplain came in and asked me to follow him. I did so and he took me up to the Memorial Chapel and

> pointed to the Memorial Tablet with my name on it. This was later taken down whilst I was on leave and my name erased.

The final part of Chief Petty Officer Sydney Kay's recollections of his time spent as a member of HMS *Turbulent*'s crew is particularly interesting. The announcement of the vessel having not made it back to port at the end of her patrol, and being officially listed as "missing", was not announced in the press until 3 May 1943. Sydney says he arrived back in the UK on the Tuesday after Whitsun, 1943. With Whitsun that year falling on Sunday, 13 June, this means Kay's return to the UK was on Tuesday, 15 June. The Admiralty did not change the status of *Turbulent* and her crew to "missing, presumed dead" until Tuesday, 21 December 1943, which raises the obvious question of why a memorial listing the names of the entire crew had already been erected when it was a further six months before the Admiralty changed their official status.

CHAPTER EIGHT

HMS *Turbulent* in the News

The following article appeared in the *Portsmouth Evening News* on Wednesday, 10 June 1942, just two months before HMS *Turbulent* attacked and damaged the Italian cargo ship MV *Nino Bixio,* which at the time was carrying Allied prisoners of war, 336 of whom were killed. A more detailed account of this incident can be found in Chapter Four "The Attack on *Nino Bixio*" earlier in this book.

Commander Linton
Submarine Sinks Convoy

H.M. Submarine *Turbulent*, under the command of Commander J. W. Linton, D.S.C., R.N., formerly a well-known United Services' Rugby player in Portsmouth, has carried out a very successful patrol in the Central Mediterranean, where she has effectively attacked the Axis supply lines to Libya.

In the course of her patrol, state the Admiralty, the *Turbulent* sank three medium sized supply ships, an

> Italian destroyer of the 1,628-ton Navigatori class, and a small merchant vessel.
>
> Two Italian destroyers were escorting two heavily laden supply ships of medium size. *Turbulent* attacked and sank not only both supply ships of this convoy, but also one of the escorting destroyers. The third supply ship which was sunk formed part of another convoy.
>
> A small merchant vessel laden with explosive was also sunk.

Turbulent's fifth war patrol took place between 11 May and 4 June 1942, and as the submarine's sixth patrol did not begin until 17 June, this article in the *Portsmouth Evening News* is clearly describing the former, which began and concluded at Alexandria, Egypt. Its orders were to patrol in the Gulf of Sirte region of the Mediterranean Sea.

Four days into its patrol, on 14 May, *Turbulent* came to the surface off Ras el Hilal in Libya and opened fire with its deck gun, sinking the Italian vessel the *San Guisto*, which had a cargo of 160 tons of fuel. This would appear to be the "small merchant vessel" referred to in the article.

It was eleven days before *Turbulent* carried out any more attacks on enemy shipping, but that was not for the want of trying. On 29 May, and whilst still off the coast of Bengasi, Commander Linton engaged and sank two Italian vessels. The first was the naval destroyer, *Emmanuelle Pessagno*, which was struck by a single torpedo, and the second being the merchant vessel the *Capo Arma*, which was struck by two of the other three torpedoes fired by *Turbulent.*

The newspaper article indicates that five enemy vessels were sunk, yet *Turbulent's* own patrol log shows that it in fact sank only four.

An article next appeared in the *Long Eaton Advertiser* newspaper on Saturday, 20 June 1942, describing a member of HMS *Turbulent*'s crew. What is interesting here is that the article gives a detailed account of some of the submarine's many actions, along with personal information about one of the crew, which would not have otherwise been widely known.

Long Eaton Petty Officer Aboard A Gallant Submarine

MADE HISTORY WITH H.M.S. *TURBULENT* ONE OF TWO BROTHERS SERVING WITH H.M. FORCES

A member of the crew of H.M. Submarine *Turbulent*, and the youngest member of the Submarine Service when he joined up two years ago, Chief Petty Officer F. Wallis, E.R.A., is a son of whom Mr and Mrs. A. W. Wallis, of 53 College Street, Long Eaton, may well be proud.

Chief Petty Officer Wallis is a native of Long Eaton and attended the Church of England Schools. He commenced work with Messrs. Crossley Premier, Sandiacre, where he achieved his ambition to become an engineer.

He had taken part in many of the actions in which the *Turbulent* has been engaged, and the exploits of this submarine make thrilling reading.

Axis planes and warships made four determined attempts to blast the submarine *Turbulent* out of the sea during a great patrol in which she sank four supply ships and an Italian destroyer. Two of the attacks came from the air, her skipper, Commander John Wallace Linton, of Gloucestershire, stated on arrival at his home base. One of these occurred in broad daylight off the Libyan coast when the submarine had surfaced. Low flying planes appeared, but the *Turbulent* crash-dived.

Cheated of Their Prey

The second attack came when the submarine was cruising on patrol at night, but again the attackers were cheated of their prey. Two undersea attacks were also unsuccessful. The surviving Italian destroyer dropped no fewer than 25 depth charges, but they failed to do any damage.

An American observer, Lieutenant Reginald Raymond, who was on board during the patrol, said, "Your Mediterranean submarines are doing a most magnificent job. We are learning a lot from you, Reginald."

Commander Linton, burly, bearded ace submarine officer, who has accounted for 11 merchant ships, two warships, and eight schooners, in his last twelve patrols, said the first ships to be sighted were two 3,000-ton merchantmen escorted by two destroyers. They were bound for Libya with supplies for Rommel's armies.

Schooner Burst Into Flames

The *Turbulent*, after approaching to within 200 yards, hit one of the destroyers and both merchant ships with torpedoes. The destroyer sank in four minutes, and a merchantman went down in ten minutes; an ammunition ship blazed for four hours then blew up.

On another night a supply ship of 3,000 to 4,000 tons, escorted by two destroyers, was hit by two torpedoes and sank. More depth charges were dropped, but the submarine again escaped. A 500-ton schooner was spotted off the Libyan coast in daylight and the *Turbulent* came to the surface and fired a dozen shells. The schooner burst into flames, was run aground by her crew and abandoned.

Honour to the Town

Chief Petty Officer Wallis is the youngest member of the crew. Long Eaton people will be proud to share with his parents the honour he has brought to the town of his birth.

Chief Petty Officer F. Wallis DSM was Frederick Charles Wallis. His service number was C/MX 64815, and the letters ERA after his name stand for Engine Room Artificer (4th Class). According to the website www.uboat.net, *Turbulent* is believed to have been sunk by depth charges when it was attacked by the Italian torpedo boat *Ardito* off Punta Licosa, south of Naples, on 6 March 1943. The Commonwealth War Graves Commission records Wallis' death as being 23 March 1943, whilst serving as a member of *Turbulent's* crew. He was 23 years of age. He has no known grave, but his name is recorded on the Chatham Naval Memorial in Kent.

The following article was taken from an undated and unnamed newspaper, believed to be from New Zealand.

> The submarine *Turbulent* is safe in its berth after sinking four Axis supply ships and an Italian destroyer in one Mediterranean patrol during which enemy planes and warships made four determined attempts to "get" her.
>
> She is commanded by Commander J. W. Linton, D.S.C., of Gloucestershire, who now has 16 enemy ships to his credit.
>
> "It was nightfall and we were on the surface," said one of the *Turbulent*'s officers. "We suddenly sighted two merchantmen escorted by two destroyers. We dared not dive because of the danger of the periscope making a splash and giving us away. So we fired four torpedoes in rapid succession and got away at top speed and dived."
>
> **"Sea Like Shambles"**
>
> "As we dived there were several loud bangs which sounded like a ship breaking up. Then there was a bang which shook us to the teeth. It was an ammunition ship exploding.
>
> "We came to the surface and saw we had sunk two merchant ships of 6,000 and 4,000 tons respectively, and also one of the two destroyers. The sea was a shambles with wreckage all round and survivors clinging to it."

> The *Turbulent*'s gunnery officer describing the sinking of a fourth Italian vessel, a 500-ton schooner said;
>
> "We sighted the two three mastered schooners at 2,000 yards and fired 15 rounds. We got nine or ten hits and then had to crash dive as aircraft were approaching."
>
> The *Turbulent* is one of a flotilla of submarines steadily blasting enemy convoys taking supplies to Rommel in Libya. The destroyer ship sunk was of the Navigator class of 1,600 tons.

The *Fleetwood Chronicle* of Friday, 19 March 1943, thirteen days after *Turbulent* was officially recorded as having been lost, carried a somewhat poignant article about an exchange of plaques which had taken place between the town of Fleetwood in Lancashire and HMS *Turbulent.*

By the date of the article, the British government and senior members of the Royal Navy would have already been aware of *Turbulent*'s missing status, information which they clearly had not shared with the national press. Yet despite this they still went ahead with the exchange, possibly because at the time the news had not been made public and was something they did not want to announce, because to do so would have informed Britain's enemies.

> ***Fleetwood and H.M.S Turbulent***
> **Town and Submarine Exchange Plaques**
>
> FLEETWOOD'S coat-of-arms plaque is now on its way to HM Submarine *Turbulent*, and the

submarine's crest plaque is to occupy an honoured place in Fleetwood Town Hall.

In the Marine Hall on Thursday night the plaques were officially exchanged.

The plaque for *Turbulent* was handed to Captain H. B. Bedwell, R N., by Ald. H. Blackburn, and the Mayor (Ald. W. H. Thompson, JP.) received the submarine's plaque from Capt. Bedwell.

Ald. T. Clegg, chairman of Fleetwood National Savings Committee, presided.

Before handing the plaque to Capt. Bedwell, Ald. Blackburn, who was Mayor during Warship Week last year, when Fleetwood invested enough to adopt the submarine, said that *Turbulent* was a wonderful submarine and had done wonderful work in the Mediterranean.

"The plaque is the only one of its kind to be presented to the Royal Navy," he said.

"It is a wonderful plaque and a wonderful piece of craftsmanship, not just carpentry."

Ald. Blackburn said the plaque was designed by Mr. C. Johnstone and made by Mr. Garnett.

"I may as well be a bit egotistical, and tell you that the idea was mine," he said.

Ald. Blackburn said he hoped that when *Turbulent* returned to a home base the Mayor would invite the crew to Fleetwood. "I will see that all expenses are paid," he said.

Accepting the plaque, Capt. Bedwell said he represented the Flag Officer-in-Charge and the Admiralty.

ALL WILL SEE IT

Capt. Bedwell said he was sorry *Turbulent*'s commanding officer could not be present. That of course was impossible.

He congratulated the designer and the craftsman responsible for the plaque.

"If there should be a Fleetwood man aboard *Turbulent*, his thoughts will be turned to his home town," he said. "If there isn't, the thoughts of those on board will turn to a town in the best country in the world. The plaque will be put in a bulkhead, where every member of the crew can see it."

Capt. Bedwell then handed *Turbulent*'s plaque to the Mayor.

What Bedwell did not clarify to the Mayor of Fleetwood and his colleagues was that the reason *Turbulent*'s commanding officer could not be present was because the submarine had been lost. In which case, the use of the word "impossible," was actually a euphemism, and had nothing to do with logistics. At the time of the ceremony, Captain Bedwell was stationed at HMS Eaglet, a Royal Naval land base in Liverpool. Five months later he became the Naval Officer-in-Charge, Fleetwood.

Harold Brisbane Bedwell, an Australian by birth, had a long and distinguished naval career, having joined the British Royal Navy on 15 January 1894, initially serving on board the armoured cruiser HMS *Immortalite* in 1896, as a Midshipman. During the First World War he took part in the Battle of Jutland as the Navigating Officer on board the cruiser HMS *Minotaur* and was Mentioned in Despatches for his actions. On 28 August 1918 he was also awarded the French Légion d'Honneur for services rendered during the war.

Having served in the Royal Navy for thirty-two years, he retired on 4 July 1926 with the rank of Captain. He was reactivated on 25 August 1939, just before the outbreak of the Second World War, by which time he was just two months shy of his sixtieth birthday. He remained in service until 30 December 1944, having served at five different Royal Naval Bases, the last one having been HMS Eaglet.

An important and interesting article appeared in the *Bradford Observer* on Tuesday, 4 May 1943; the first official announcement that HMS *Turbulent*, and its entire crew, were presumed to be lost at sea.

H.M. Submarine "Turbulent" Lost

> An Admiralty communique last night states: "The Board of Admiralty regret to announce that H.M. submarine *Turbulent* (Commander J. W. Linton, D.S.O., D.S.C., R.N.), is overdue and must be presumed lost. Next of kin of casualties have been informed."

> Commander Linton was estimated to have sunk 27 enemy ships, and recent sinkings may have brought his score level with that of "ace" submarine commander, Ben Bryant, who had sunk 29 ships up to the end of February.

Commander Bryant went on to become the Royal Navy's greatest surviving submarine ace of the Second World War, having been officially recognised as being responsible for the sinking of a total of thirty-two enemy ships.

At the outbreak of the war he was a Lieutenant Commander aboard HMS *Sealion*, an S-class submarine of the Royal Navy, a position he held until 12 October 1941. He then took command of HMS *Safari*, his last submarine command, which was a newer and more up to date S-class submarine, with whom he served with until 27 April 1943. For his wartime service Bryant was awarded the Distinguished Service Order with two bars, the Distinguished Service Cross, and was also Mentioned in Despatches.

By May 1943, news of *Turbulent's* demise and the loss of its entire crew was common knowledge. One man, Mr F. Oleander Lewis, was so moved by the losses that he felt compelled to write to the editor of his local newspaper on the matter. His letter appeared in the *Fleetwood Chronicle* on Friday, 14 May 1943.

Night Life

> Sir,
>
> With the waters of the Mediterranean as a tomb, lie brave commander and crew of Fleetwood's adopted submarine, *Turbulent*. They gave their lives that we might live; they died in the fight for a better world.

It was stated in your paper last week that all Fleetwood was shocked. Well, judging by some events this week, some people soon recovered.

I took a walk through the town a few nights ago just as the public houses and clubs were closing. Crowds of people, young and old, of both sexes were hanging about the exits, evidently loath to leave. In several cases, arguments between drunken persons were taking place, language which was more vivid than decent was rife. In more than one place I saw objectionable messes caused by people having taken more alcohol than they could hold.

In the main street a fight was in progress between six or seven drunken contestants. Here again, lewd language was being used freely. A large crowd had collected, and the spectators, to my way of thinking, seemed neither angry nor shocked, as some of them emphatically discouraged some soldiers who attempted to stop the fight. An elderly lady was knocked down by a sudden movement of the crowd.

On the following night I was in a public bar, crowded with people spending money like water. A man came in and loudly advertised for sale 25 clothing coupons; a well-dressed, well-fed, bejewelled woman was proudly displaying a wristlet-watch which she said a man friend had purchased for her for £75.

You suggested that we pay homage to those of the *Turbulent* by subscribing money to buy a new submarine. To give or lend a little of our filthy lucre

> is not enough. Let us also do our bit towards getting that better world which these brave, unselfish men gave their lives to obtain.

Mr Lewis's letter could be described as somewhat confusing. It was wartime after all. Ships were lost at sea, aircraft were shot down, civilians were killed in bombing raids, and somewhere in the world soldiers were being killed nearly every day. People tended to live for the moment just in case it was their turn next. It is more than likely that the people Mr Lewis talks about in his letter were doing nothing more outlandish than simply getting on with their lives.

The *Hartlepool Northern Daily Mail* of Tuesday, 30 November 1943, included the following article:

PRESUMED LOST

> Mr. W. Hall, of 15 Bertha Street, has been officially informed that his son, Stoker (First Class) Richard Hall (23) of H.M. submarine *Turbulent*, who was reported missing in March this year, is now presumed lost. Stoker Hall was an old boy of Church Square School, and had been in the Navy for more than 3 years.

It must have been extremely difficult for families such as the Halls, who lost loved ones when *Turbulent* was sunk. Not knowing whether his son was alive or dead not only left him in some kind of slow-motion limbo, but it must also have been extremely stressful. Each day of the eight months Mr Hall had to wait for confirmation that his son was officially dead (rather than missing) would have been a constant mental battle of trying to convince himself that "no news was good news", and that the longer he heard nothing from the authorities increased the chances that his son, Richard, had survived the sinking of HMS *Turbulent*. Sadly for Mr Hall, all remaining hope for him was dashed at the end of November 1943, when the authorities finally confirmed *Turbulent*'s fate.

Another Hartlepool resident who received similar news to Mr Hall was Mrs Barbara Bromby, who was informed about the loss of her husband, Chief Engine Room Artificer P/MX 50465 Harry Bromby (DSM). The couple had a young daughter named Anne.

The crew of HMS *Turbulent* were not exclusively from one particular area. However, it is clear that some towns and cities, in this case Hartlepool, lost more than just one of their brave young men when the submarine disappeared in 1943.

The *Aberdeen Press and Journal* from Wednesday, 22 December 1943 carried news concerning the loss of *Turbulent*'s crew. The article appeared nine months after it is believed the submarine was actually lost, and a day after the Admiralty had officially listed the entire crew as "missing presumed dead". The suspected loss of HMS *Turbulent* had originally been announced by the Admiralty on 5 May 1943, which in itself was some two months after the submarine's believed disappearance.

Presumed Lost
CREW OF SUBMARINE TURBULENT

The entire crew of the submarine *Turbulent*, the loss of which was announced on May 3, were yesterday posted officially as "missing presumed dead".

> Six officers and sixty-one ratings are named in an Admiralty casualty list.
>
> The officers are headed by Cmdr. J. W. Linton, V.C., D.S.O., D.S.C., who was in command when he was given the V.C. on May 25. It was stated that it was not a posthumous award, for at the time the officers and crew were posted as "missing".

The citation for the award of his Victoria Cross made mention of an attack carried out by *Turbulent* on the night of 28/29 May 1942. Linton had previously been awarded the Distinguished Service Cross on 6 May 1941, whilst serving as a Lieutenant Commander on board the submarine HMS *Pandora*, "For courage and determination in sinking two Italian supply ships." On 15 September 1942, whilst Commander of the *Turbulent*, he was appointed a Companion of the Distinguished Service Order, "For courage and skill in successful submarine patrols in HMS *Turbulent*."

> One of Britain's most daring submarine "aces", Cmdr. Linton was constantly in command of submarines from the outbreak of war until *Turbulent*'s last patrol.
>
> One cruiser, one destroyer, one U-boat, twenty-eight supply ships, some 100,000 tons in all, were sunk by his "subs". He also destroyed three trains by gunfire. He was thirty-seven and lived at Warminster.
>
> Other officers named include Lt. J. P. Blake and Lt. B. C. W. Clements, both of whom received the D.S.C. for bravery and devotion to duty in the *Turbulent*.

> Cmdr. John Wallace Linton joined the submarine service in 1927 and was our oldest submarine commander. Repeatedly he refused a shore appointment and remained a great fighter, the "happy warrior" of the submarine service.
>
> His wife Nancy and his sons Bill and Jim, lived until recently at Merseyhampton, near Fairfield, Gloucestershire, the county of his birth.

King George VI presented Commander Linton's Victoria Cross to his widow Nancy and two sons, William and James, at an investiture which took place at Buckingham Palace in February 1944. An article about the event appeared in the *Newcastle Evening Chronicle* of Friday, 25 February 1944.

The King Honours Dead Heroes

> Four V.C.s and three George Crosses awarded posthumously were among decorations, numbering over 160, presented to next-of-kin by the King at a recent Buckingham Palace investiture.
>
> Fourteen-year-old William Linton received the V.C. and D.S.O. won by his father, Cmdr. John Linton, R.N., Captain of Submarine Turbulent, in May.

Linton's elder son William attended the investiture wearing naval uniform, as despite his age, he had already decided to follow in his father's footsteps and serve in the Royal Navy. A sad footnote to this story is that William Linton not only followed his father as a submariner, but also died whilst serving on the A-class HMS *Affray*, which was lost at sea on 16 April 1951. It remains the last vessel of the Royal Navy to be lost in such a manner.

It would appear that *Turbulent*, its commanding officer, and the submarine's crew, were highly thought of by the Admiralty, as they were extremely keen to promote their successful attacks on enemy shipping at every opportunity. Reading through these articles one could almost be left wondering whether the promotional aspect was aimed more at Linton rather than *Turbulent*, as no matter the submarine, it was the captain's skills and abilities which ultimately determined how effective it was.

There is, of course, the question as to why it took nearly nine months for the Admiralty to officially confirm the loss of *Turbulent* and its crew. It is more than likely that the announcement about its loss was delayed purely to keep Axis nations guessing as to whether or not it had actually been sunk.

CHAPTER NINE

Official Documents from The National Archives

Forty-five documents concerning the loss of HMS *Turbulent* can be found in The National Archives. They make for interesting reading as well as shedding some light on the "behind the scenes" activities carried out by the naval authorities that were considered routine in such circumstances.

The documents have been included here to help provide a detailed narrative about what actions were taken by the British naval authorities in the days and weeks after *Turbulent* failed to return from what was its last war patrol. Collectively, these documents help to paint a fuller picture of what went on in the background when such incidents took place.

The Casualty Action Sheet was an official and sequential checklist of eleven actions that needed to be carried out after *Turbulent* failed to return from its patrol on 23 March. The list culminated with the sending out of condolence letters to the crews' immediate next of kin. The first entry on the form is dated 24 March 1943, and the last 12 December 1943.

Point #3 on the document is under the heading "treatment of casualty". It is dated 26 March 1943 and shows that at that time, certain members of the crew were officially listed as being missing because notifications were sent out to the naval bases at Chatham, Devonport and Portsmouth with instructions for them to send out "confidential letters" to their next of kin informing them of the status of their loved ones. This was completed by 1 April. Having failed to return from its patrol as anticipated on 23 March, it was clear that something had happened and had resulted in the loss of both the vessel and crew. The notifications sent out to next of kin were just a week after *Turbulent* failed to return from patrol.

Point #9 ensured that *Turbulent's* crew list, at the time of leaving Algiers on 23 February 1943, on what would turn out to be its final war patrol, was correct, so that letters would not be sent out to families of the wrong men.

Point #10 concerns whether the time had come to consider "presumption of death" letters in relation to the crew. A report was sent to the Ministry of Defence on 6 November, which was approved on 19 November, with the letters being sent out to next of kin on 6 December.

Point #11 covers letters of condolence sent out to the next of kin by King George VI. This took place between 1 and 6 December. Of these, twenty-three were posted from the naval base at Chatham, nineteen were posted from Portsmouth, and eighteen from Devonport. Rather than sending the letters from a central location as might be expected in such circumstances, they were instead sent from the naval bases where the men had carried out their initial training.

The Official Admiralty Communique, Serial No. 311, is a 3-page document listing the "Officers" and "Ratings" on board. Although none of the pages is dated, the list of names must have been compiled after 25 May 1943, as this was the day Commander John Wallace Linton was awarded the Victoria Cross and the letters VC are included after his name on the list. Other crew members also have the awards they received at the same time as Commander Linton was awarded his VC recorded after their surnames.

The following is a correspondence between the Admiralty and the Royal Navy's Press Division over the release of a photograph that appeared in the press, purporting to show HMS *Turbulent* returning to port after the end of its last patrol, despite the fact that the submarine had already been officially reported as missing. The appearance of such an image would have no doubt caused both stress and confusion to the relatives and next of kin of the submarine's crew.

Press Division

> Following the recent publication in the Press of the picture of H.M.S/M Turbulent returning to port, several bitter letters have been received at R.N Barracks, Devonport, criticising the Admiralty for the production of the photograph.
>
> No doubt many more letters in a similar strain will be received at the Depots and the Admiralty, and it will be necessary to inform the writers of the circumstances in which the picture was published.
>
> As it is understood that the Admiralty is in no way responsible for this unfortunate error, will D.P.D

(Director of Press Division) please indicate the nature of the reply to be made.

Signed F. Broughton
C.W. (C)
April 1943

The photographs in question were issued to the M.O.I (Ministry of Information) on 22 March, at which time nothing was known in the Press Division of HMS *Turbulent*'s loss.

(2). The Admiralty has no control over the date of issue of photographs, and it is very much regretted that the Ministry Photographic Division did not issue these until 6/4/43. D.P.D. has already pointed out to the Ministry how unfortunate this delay was.

(3). It is suggested that any enquiries concerning the publication of these photographs should be replied to on the lines that the Admiralty referred the photographs to the M.O.I. for release to the Press some time ago but unfortunately they were not published until the 6th April, and the Admiralty were not aware of the M.O.I.'s intention to publish on that date.

(4). Steps have been taken to prevent a recurrence of this regrettable mistake.

Commander, C. H. A Brooking
Director of Press Division
9th April 1943.

On 22 December 1943, an article appeared in *The Times* announcing the loss of HMS *Turbulent* and its crew:

> **H.M.S. Turbulent**
>
> The board of enquiry regrets to announce the following casualties sustained in H.M. submarine *Turbulent*, the loss of which has already been announced. Next of kin have been notified.

The article then included a complete list of the officers and men who were lost with HMS *Turbulent.* This list appears in the appendices in the back of this book.

The wife of a crewman on HMS *Turbulent*, Mrs Elizabeth Ford, sent a letter to the Admiralty. The letter is dated 25 September 1944.

> Dear Sir,
>
> I enclose a photo cut from a recent *Daily Sketch* and the fellow marked with a cross, bears a very great resemblance to my husband, presumed dead on the submarine H.M.S *Turbulent*, lost in 1943.
>
> Can you help me in any way, or could you put me in touch with any survivors of this submarine which would help me a great deal in my anxiety. Any news however small would be gratefully received.
>
> Thanking you for a speedy reply
> Sincerely
> E. Ford

A reply to Mrs Ford was sent from the Admiralty in London. It is dated 16 October 1944.

> Madam,
>
> In reply to your letter of 25th September, I am commanded by My Lords Commissioners of the Admiralty to inform you that H.M. submarine TURBULENT in which your husband Cyril D. Ford, A.B., C/JX.19948 was serving, was lost in the Tyrrhenian Sea in March 1943. No survivors have been reported and death has been formally presumed for all the officers and men on board.
>
> (2). Having regard to the fact that the surrounding territory was at that time in enemy occupation it is considered unlikely that any survivor could have reached France.
>
> (3). In these circumstances My Lords are of the opinion that the person shown in the photograph cannot be your husband.
>
> (4). The newspaper cutting is returned herewith.
>
> I am, Madam,
> Your obedient servant
> J. G. Lang

It was not uncommon for wives or parents of servicemen to contact military authorities concerning the official status of their loved ones when ambiguities existed as to whether they were alive or dead. There were many occasions when families were informed that a relative was missing in action, which in effect left them in limbo, especially the longer that status remained in place. These were extremely sensitive and emotional situations, often resulting in family members grabbing hold of the slightest glimmer of hope that their loved one might still be alive. Mrs Elizabeth Ford was just one such relative.

Next is what looks like a fax message and concerns a mother who had not received the original notification of her son's death. Sadly, it is undated, but was sent from the Royal Navy base at Chatham.

From Combrax Chatham
to
Captain (S) V Fort Blockhouse

W A Glester, A B C/SSX 32771 Missing Turbulent.

N O Kin, Mother Mrs Hopson at 94 St Stephen's Road, East Ham, London E.6., states she did not receive the original notification.

She has now been notified by letter today 8th May. Request casualty return be amended.

William Arthur Glester was a 22-year-old Able Seaman at the time of his death. His name is commemorated on the Chatham Naval Memorial. William had been awarded the Distinguished Service Medal, as well as having been Mentioned in Despatches during his time serving in the navy.

The announcement for William having been Mentioned in Despatches appeared in the *London Gazette*, on Friday, 11 November 1942.

The award of William's Distinguished Service Medal "for bravery and devotion to duty in successful patrols in H.M.S. Turbulent", was announced in the *London Gazette* newspaper on Friday, 21 May 1943. Although awarded after his death, it was not a posthumous award.

The next of kin for all members of HMS *Turbulent*'s crew received a copy of a standard letter from the Royal Naval Barracks where they were stationed, which in this case included Chatham, Devonport and Portsmouth. Although a standard letter, it would have been extremely personal to those families who were unfortunate enough to receive one.

> Dear ....
>
> With reference to my letter of yesterday's date concerning the sad death of your .... If you wish to enquire whether you are eligible for a pension you should apply to the Chief Regional Officer, Ministry of Pensions, whose address can be obtained from any Post Office. Delay will result where application is made otherwise than to the Chief Regional Officer.
>
> Should you have been dependent upon him and be in immediate need of assistance, I suggest that you apply to the Secretary, R.N. Benevolent Trust, "Glenthorne," Kingston Crescent, Portsmouth, if you are resident in the County of Hampshire, otherwise, to the Secretary of the nearest branch of the Soldiers,

Sailors' and Airmen's Families Association whose address can be obtained at any Post Office, (or from 23, Queen Anne's Gate, Westminster), or direct in writing to the General Secretary, R.N. Benevolent Trust, 10, New Road Rochester, Kent.

If you were in receipt of an Allotments and Dependent's Allowance, payment thereof will be continued for a limited period, and you will receive a communication on this subject from the Director of Navy Accounts in the course of a few days. This payment will be in the nature of an advance on account of any pension which you may be awarded and will be taken into consideration in the event of such award.

Any application you may have to make concerning his estate should be made by letter to the Inspector of Seamen's Wills, Admiralty, Foxhill Hutments, Combe Down, Bath. [The next four lines of this paragraph have been redacted but appear to mention wills and the obtaining of uniform, kit and personal belongings.]

A CERTIFICATE OF DEATH can be obtained free of charge on application direct to the director of Navy accounts, Branch 3, Foxhill Hutments, Combe Down, Bath.

If you require any help in completing any of your application forms I shall be only too pleased to assist you.

The Commonwealth War Graves records the names of 107,616 members of the Royal Navy who died throughout the years of the Second World War, meaning that this would have been a letter that was sent out to an extremely large number of people by the end of the conflict.

A message stamped **Most Secret** in red ink was the next document I read through and is a timeline of events from when *Turbulent* left its base in Algiers.

Important

Regret to report TURBULENT overdue from patrol and must be considered lost.

(2). Turbulent left Algiers 24th February to patrol south of 40 degrees, and east of 14 degrees, from 28th February to p.m. 6th March and then north of 40 degrees east and 13 degrees until pm 12th.

(3). TURBULENT was ordered to leave pm 12th March and proceed toward Giglio Island then across to east coast or Corsica and to report in due course his E.T.A. south east of Sardinia for homeward route. I expected this to be about 18th March, but no report from TURBULENT was received.

(4). TURBULENT was ordered to patrol in a position about 40 miles off east coast of Sardinia from 2100/19th March to 0001/20th then to withdraw and report E.T.A. south east of Sardinia. No reply was received.

(5). On 20th was given onward route to Algiers to arrive 0630 today and to acknowledge. No reply was received.

(6). TURBULENT was sighted off Bonifati on 1st March and also off east coast of Corsica on 14th March.

(7). In absence of enemy claims I am of the opinion TURBULENT was mined on or after 14th March possibly in the vicinity of Maddalena. (Note circumstances attending loss of P. 311).

(8). The grievous loss of this outstanding submarine on her last patrol before proceeding to U.K. to refit is most keenly felt. Report in amplification follows.

(9). C. in C. Levant pass to S.1. V.A. Malta pass to S.10.

It is interesting to note in point seven of this report that the officially held belief at the time was that HMS *Turbulent* was lost on or after 14 March 1943, near Maddalena. This archipelago is situated on the northern tip of Sardinia, hundreds of miles away from Tabarka, where amateur diver Jean-Pierre Misson claims the wreck of HMS *Turbulent* lays. (See Chapter 12)

It struck me that if *Turbulent* was not in fact sunk off Maddalena on 14 March, as officialdom would have us believe, and instead made her way down the east coast of Sardinia, the final leg of the journey back to its base at Algiers would not have required the submarine to have gone anywhere near

Tabarka. Having reached the southern tip of Sardinia, there was then a direct south-westerly route back to her base.

What is clear from reading through the documents held by The National Archives is that there is no absolute certainty about what happened to HMS *Turbulent*.

CHAPTER TEN

Ultra-Secret Intelligence

In relation to military intelligence, the classification of "Ultra Secret" was used because the quality and importance of the information obtained was so good that it was deemed to be higher than the previous highest level of security classification, "Top Secret".

Ultra was first used by British Military Intelligence in June 1941 and remained in use throughout the rest of the war. In essence it was one of the most formidable weapons the Allied powers had in their possession and would prove essential in the battle against German U-boats in the Atlantic, as well as aiding and assisting Allied vessels in the Mediterranean. Little did the German, Italian and even Japanese know that the high-level encrypted messages they were sending amongst themselves were also being intercepted by British code breakers at Bletchley Park.

Bletchley had been used by the Government Code and Cypher School since 1938 and included some of the country's finest analytical minds. These civilian code breakers, including the likes of Alan Turing, worked tirelessly to decrypt intercepted messages by Germany's military intelligence, the Abwehr. During the course of the war the number of people who worked at Bletchley Park and its satellite stations was somewhere in the region of 10,000. Indeed, it has been estimated in certain historical quarters that the work carried out by the code breakers at Bletchley Park was so important that it helped reduce the length of the war by some two years, saving thousands of lives in the process, on both sides, both military and civilian alike.

The workers at Bletchley Park had to cope with thousands of messages being transmitted every single day, and this was just by Nazi Germany alone. The encrypted messages varied in their content between detailed military reports to and from the front line of different army groups, troop movements, movements of German merchant shipping, even down to weather reports.

As early as 1932, Marian Rejewski, a member of the Polish Cipher Bureau, had managed to decipher the workings of the Enigma machines used by German military units. Those used by the army had three barrels, while those used by the navy had four. Rejewski did not, however, achieve this breakthrough all of his own volition. The French Secret Service had provided him with copies of an up-to-date Enigma operating manual, which had been a great help.

By intercepting German radio transmissions, Rejewski was able to come up with a process which ultimately allowed him to read and understand the messages. This continued until the beginning of the war and the occupation of Poland by Nazi forces, by which time all of Rejewski's work was handed over to the British authorities. But before this priceless "gift" from Poland could properly bear fruit for its new owners, it became obsolete, as in 1940, Germany, without any knowledge that the Polish had been intercepting their military messages for the best part of six years, changed the workings of their Enigma machines, which in turn eliminated the breakthrough Rejewski had previously managed to achieve.

The British, far from being dejected, set their cryptologists, mathematicians and scientists at Bletchley Park to work on the dilemma. An early breakthrough by these determined individuals allowed the work which Rejewski had begun to continue, but this was only in relation to the German army and the Luftwaffe.

Eaves-dropping German naval communications had still proved somewhat elusive, as the Enigma system used was slightly different. This was a massive problem for the British because it was at this early stage of the war when so much merchant shipping, carrying much needed supplies from the United States, was being lost in the Atlantic to German U-boats. This was also extremely problematic for Royal Navy submarines, who were also at the mercy of the U-boats.

There was much concern with the continued German successes, with some observers believing that if a lack of foodstuffs continued to fail to arrive, Britain would be left with no other solution than to surrender.

A turning point in the worth and value of intelligence was greatly affected by two events which took place in 1941, both of which resulted in the capture of intact, workable Enigma sets recovered from captured German U-boats.

The type IXB German submarine *U-110* was captured on 9 May 1941. Having been commissioned by the *Kriegsmarine* on 21 November 1940, it was on its second war patrol when it attacked the British convoy O.B.318, which had left Scotland at about 2100 on Wednesday, 7 May 1941. The massive convoy consisted of thirty-eight vessels and was en route for ports along the North American coastline.

U-110 attacked the convoy in the North Atlantic firing three torpedoes which sank two of the British vessels. Before the German submarine could fire its fourth torpedo, it was spotted by escorting vessels of the convoy and attacked with depth charges by the destroyers HMS *Bulldog* and *Broadway*, and the corvette HMS *Aubretia*.

Having been forced to surface, a short gun battle took place, resulting in the death of fourteen of the submarine's forty-seven officers and crew. When it became apparent that his submarine was about to be rammed and possibly sunk by HMS *Bulldog*, the commanding officer of *U-110*, Kapitanleutnant Fritz Julius Lemp, ordered his crew to abandon ship, which they did by jumping into the water. Once he realised his vessel was not going to be rammed and that the Enigma equipment might well fall into enemy hands, Lemp began swimming back to his submarine, presumably to destroy his Enigma set. He never made it. There are differing stories about what happened, but the likeliest version is that he was shot by the British when they realised there must be something on board that he did not want to fall into British hands.

HMS *Bulldog* quickly made its way to the stricken *U-110* and pulled alongside. The British submarine's commanding officer, Sub Lieutenant David Balme, led a boarding party to search the stricken German submarine. Its capture, although perhaps not fully appreciated at the time, was probably one of the most significant events of the entire war thanks to the Enigma machine, codebooks and other related documentation found on board.

Balme and his men took their time with their search. They were thorough to the extreme and made a number of journeys to remove any items they believed may have had some kind of intelligence value, as well as a few souvenirs no doubt as well.

Thankfully for the Allies, some of the recovered documents also helped the codebreakers at Bletchley Park to solve *Reservehandverfahren*, a reserve German hand cipher.

It was only Lemp who knew the significance of the equipment on board. None of his crew was aware. It was only the day after the capture of *U-110*, once the items removed had been fully examined, that its real significance was fully understood by the Admiralty in London. This in turn caused the British a problem because it was soon clear that they could not allow the Germans to discover they had not only captured one of their submarines, but also recovered an Enigma set and associated documents from it. If the Germans discovered what had transpired, they would have immediately changed their codes and cipher systems to their Enigma sets, in essence meaning the one the British had gone to so much effort to recover was of absolutely no use. With this in mind, *U-110* was allowed to sink.

The next question was what to do with the captured German crew, as well as their own men from HMS *Bulldog*. The solution to the latter was relatively straight forward; they were sworn to secrecy and threatened with prosecution under the Official Secrets Act if they so much as uttered a word about what they knew. As for the surviving crew members of *U-110*, they were taken to Iceland where they were securely interned until the end of the war. It is more than likely that the Admiralty did not inform their German counterparts that thirty-two of their men were being held as prisoners of war, instead simply letting them believe that the submarine, along with all its crew, had been lost when it failed to return to its home base at the end of its patrol.

The German submarine *U-570* was commissioned in the *Kriegsmarine's* 3rd Submarine Flotilla, on 15 May 1941, under the command of Kapitanleutnant Hans-Joachim Rahmlow. It was on its first war patrol when it was attacked and damaged by an RAF Lockheed Hudson bomber aircraft of No. 269 Squadron in the North Sea, on 27 August 1941. The damage sustained by the U-boat was not sufficient to sink it, but it was certainly enough to prevent it from diving, which in essence meant that it had become a surface vessel and was now at the mercy of whatever the British wanted to throw at it. What is remarkable about this incident is that it was the first and only time during the war that a German U-boat surrendered to an aircraft.

The first Royal naval vessel to reach *U-570*'s location later that same evening was the anti-submarine trawler HMT *Northern Chief.* During the early hours of the following morning, more vessels arrived, including the Royal Navy destroyer HMS *Burwell*, a Canadian destroyer HMCS *Niagra*, and an armed trawler *Kingston Agate.* A tow line was eventually attached to *U-570* and the Allied vessels then slowly started making their way towards Iceland with a number of Hudson and Catalina aircraft securing the skies above. The intention was to take it to the capital, Reykjavik, but it ended up being beached two days after its capture, at Porlakshofn, which was a much shorter distance. All forty-four members of the boat's crew survived the ordeal.

On 31 August, British submarine commander Lieutenant George Robson Colvin, a team of Royal Navy engineers and civilian technical experts who had been flown to Iceland from the UK, boarded *U-570* to carry out a thorough examination of the vessel. The crew of the submarine had either not had sufficient time, or simply had not thought to destroy any important documents and paperwork. This included copies of encrypted signals along with German text, which proved extremely useful to the British scientists who were part of the Enigma code breaking unit at Bletchley Park. Possibly even more significant was the discovery of the U-boat commander's handbook, which provided both context and information for decrypted messages. This included abbreviations and jargon which previous to this the British had been unfamiliar with, and which had made German naval communications difficult to interpret and understand.

The vessel was salvaged and on 5 October 1941, it came into service with the Royal Navy as HMS *Graph*, before finally being decommissioned on 21 June 1943.

In June 1941 the team at Bletchley Park finally managed to begin decoding messages used by the German *Kriegsmarine* on a daily basis, with the help of their own code making machines known as Bombes.

The success achieved at Bletchley Park had to be carefully managed so as not to alert the Germans to the fact that their Enigma intelligence codes had been cracked. It was an unenviable juggling act and one which had to be maintained at all costs.

The work undertaken by those employed by the British government at Bletchley Park, along with the results they achieved, cannot be heralded enough. Each of the Enigma machines used by the Germans and the messages they sent literally had billions of possible combinations, and to keep the system safe, or so they thought, each machine was reset each and every day at midnight.

It took the combined intelligence and concentration of all those who worked tirelessly to ensure that Ultra remained as effective as it was.

It would be difficult to state with any degree of certainty exactly how many Allied vessels and men were directly saved by the information gathered by Ultra. What can be said is that during the Battle of the Mediterranean, which took place between 10 June 1940 and 2 May 1945, the Allies lost a total of seventy-six surface vessels of differing descriptions, along with forty-six submarines. The Italians lost eighty-three warships as well as eighty-three submarines, whilst Germany lost seventeen warships and sixty-eight submarines. It is quite noticeable that it was the Allies who lost far fewer submarines, especially when German and Italian losses are taken together. These numbers alone are a good indicator of the effectiveness of Ultra intercepts throughout the Mediterranean.

CHAPTER ELEVEN

The North Africa Campaign in Parliament

The purpose of this chapter is to provide an overall picture of the situation throughout the Mediterranean Sea during the time *Turbulent* was patrolling its waters. By doing this, it puts *Turbulent's* part in to a fuller and more complete perspective, and also underlines the fact that decisions made in real time were done so with numerous factors needing to be considered. Some of these decisions directly or indirectly had an effect on *Turbulent.* If just one British submarine was lost it could mean another having to be diverted from its original orders to replace it. This change would ultimately place the new submarine into a position that it would not have otherwise found itself, and which could potentially have resulted in its subsequent loss.

In most cases, when a submarine was lost this also meant the loss of the commander and the entire crew. The experience of these men individually and collectively was not something that was easy to replace. This was certainly true with the loss of HMS *Turbulent.*

On Wednesday, 3 March 1943, a statement was made in Parliament by the First Lord of the Admiralty, Mr Albert Victor Alexander, relating to the situation in the waters of the Mediterranean Sea off North Africa, including both merchant and militarily shipping. The statement focused mainly on the losses inflicted upon enemy shipping, and caused much in the way of debate amongst those present.

> In this war the enemy has had to supply some of his armed forces by sea, especially in North Africa. This has given our submarines an opportunity to inflict heavy losses. How powerful this weapon is in the hands of our young men requires no emphasis. Almost daily, the communiques issued tell of the destruction of enemy men-of-war, U-boats and shipping, wrought by the immaculate courage and high endeavour of our submarine crews. Less in number compared with the Enemy, faced with the grim necessity of searching out their targets on the enemy's coastline and in his very harbours, they ceaselessly carry out their exacting task with wonderful success. In addition, they carry on for us the training, the important training, of our own anti-submarine escorts and destroyers and may I remind the House that when dire need arose during the sustenance of Malta, they became underwater transports for the relief of the fortress.
>
> All this is not done without bitter losses but the gaps are more than filled. The increasingly large part played by the gallant officers and men of the Reserve, R.N.R and R.N.V.R., and ratings entered for hostilities only, help to ensure that our submarines go from strength

> to strength. I would add that the standard of design and construction of our submarines is proved to be second to none.
>
> The standard of training of the submarine officers and men is maintained at a very high level. In the submarine service such officers as the late Commander Wanklyn VC, and Commander Miers VC, are household names.

Lieutenant Commander Malcolm David Wanklyn VC DSO & Two Bars, who is mentioned previously in Chapter Six, was responsible for the sinking of twenty-four enemy vessels between 18 July 1940 and 19 March 1942. The date of his believed death is recorded as 14 April 1942, in line with the date he was due to have returned from patrol, but he never arrived. The actual circumstances of his death have never been confirmed. By the end of the war, Wanklyn remained the nation's most prolific destroyer of enemy vessels in a tonnage sense.

> I feel that where all have done so well, it would be invidious to make special mention of any. But the House might like me to put on record the names of a few Commanding Officers of submarines who have operated in the North African campaign and who between them have sunk a very large number indeed of enemy supply ships and their escorts. Here are the names:
>
> - Commander J. W. Linton
> - Lieutenant H. S. Mackenzie
> - Lieutenant L. W. A. Bennington

- Lieutenant P. R. H. Harrison
- Lieutenant S. L. C. Maydon
- Lieutenant A. C. G. Mars
- Lieutenant J. S. Stevens
- Lieutenant E. T. Stanley
- Lieutenant I. L. M. McGeoch

Rear Admiral Sir Murray Sueter, the Conservative MP for Hertford, was not a man concerned in any way when it came to ruffling a few feathers. In 1917 he was posted to Italy to command the Royal Naval Air Service, after having clashed with senior figures at the Admiralty. Proving that he was not a man to be trifled with, he wrote directly to King George VI. On discovering what he had done, the Sea Lords, who in essence were the Board of the Admiralty, relieved him of his command and retired him from the service with the rank of Rear Admiral.

In response to Mr Alexander's statement, Rear Admiral Sueter asked the following question of the First Lord of the Admiralty.

> Who is dealing with this U-boat menace? I asked the Prime Minister a question not long ago, and he told me that he had scrapped the Battle of the Atlantic Committee and had set up a new Committee called the U-boat Committee. Who is serving on that U-boat Committee? There is the Prime Minister. Everybody in this House will agree that the Prime Minister is very much overworked. I had the privilege of working with the Prime Minister in the last war and I know his capacity for work. He works extremely hard, but his colleagues ought to advise

him not to do quite so much. Every Member of this House hopes that the Prime Minister will soon be restored to his normal health. On that Committee, next to the Prime Minister, you have the Minister of Aircraft Production. He is one of the brain-waves of the party above the Gangway, but I do not think he knows much about submarines. Next to him, we have the First Lord of the Admiralty. He is an expert in many things, I know, but I would not quite say that he is a submarine expert. You have the Minister of Production; he is not a submarine expert. Next you have the First Sea Lord, Admiral Sir Dudley Pound. He is a very great admiral and naval strategist. In his younger days he was a torpedo officer and was an expert on the Whitehead Torpedo, but he was not a submarine officer. After the First Sea Lord, you have the Secretary of State for Air. He is a great man in the Air Service but he is not a submarine expert. There is the Minister of War Transport, he is not a submarine expert, and the Chief of the Air Staff, who is a great airman but is not a submarine expert. You have no submarine expert at all on that Committee.

The Germans have lately appointed Admiral Donetz, a U-boat ace, to take charge of the whole of the German Navy and we may expect the U-boat warfare to be intensified. I ask the First Lord to consult the Prime Minister and his colleagues to see whether they cannot put a flag officer with submarine experience in charge of the whole of the U-boat warfare. Give him some of the submarine officers who have done so well in the Mediterranean on his

> staff, and also officers from the Coastal Command, and ask the President of the United States whether he can send representatives, submarine and air experts, to serve on this committee. I am certain that we have to tackle the submarine warfare in a big way. It is no good thinking in terms of 50; we must think in terms of 500. We have also to see that we have first priority in long distance aircraft for fighting the German aircraft that work with the U-boats and aircraft for auxiliary aircraft carriers, and of radio location instruments and so on. I ask the First Lord to tell us before the Debate is over whether he has got first priority for the equipment I have mentioned. I was very glad to hear the First Lord pay such a very high tribute to our submarine service; they have done magnificent work.

In response, Mr Alexander gave the following reply:

> I am sure that my hon. and gallant Friend will remember, in view of what he said, that Admiral Sir Max Horton, who is now in charge of the main area of U-boats in the Western Command, is a very great submarine expert, and his advice and presence whenever required are available to the U-boat Committee. We take into account a great deal of what he advises.

Rear Admiral Sueter, clearly not satisfied with Alexander's reply, pushed the matter further.

Yes, I know. He is in control of the Western Command. I want a submarine officer of flag rank, and of great experience, to be in charge of the whole of Submarine Warfare. We have, I am certain, to pull up our socks over this and do more. It is no good being satisfied with what is being done. These enemy submarines are increasing in numbers and we have to face up to them; if not, we shall get a crack in this country which will be serious.

I was saying that I was very glad that the First Lord paid such a high tribute to our submarine service and to the wonderful work our submarine captains have done, particularly in the Mediterranean. All old pioneers of the submarine are thrilled when we see accounts in the Press that they have sunk ship after ship and so on, and it must give Admiral Sir Reginald Bacon great satisfaction to see what is being done in that service, the foundations of which he laid so well over 40 years ago.

CHAPTER TWELVE

Searching for the Wreck of HMS *Turbulent*

In January 2018 it was announced in a number of British newspapers that Jean-Pierre Misson, a 78-year-old amateur diver from Belgium, had discovered six Royal Navy submarines, including one he claimed was the wreckage of HMS *Turbulent*, in an area between Tabarka and Cap Negro, off the Tunisian coast, all of which had been lost during the Second World War. By then this information was somewhere in the region of three to four years old and related to sonar located discoveries made by Jean-Pierre in 2014/2015.

Jean-Pierre has been kind enough to provide documentation and information concerning his initial discoveries and subsequent investigations to attempt to confirm his findings. The inclusion of this information here does not attempt to endorse or dispute these findings, but rather it helps keep the narrative surrounding the loss of HMS *Turbulent*, along with the other missing Royal Navy vessels, alive, and ensures that healthy debate on the matter continues in the hope that it will eventually result in the discovery of the final resting place of HMS *Turbulent*.

According to Jean-Pierre, the sonar scans taken off Tabarka include a vessel with a port side, rear oriented torpedo tube, indicating, he says, that the image captured at a depth of 65 metres is that of a T-class submarine, and that the only such submarine of that class to have been in the area at the time was HMS *Turbulent.*

If Jean-Pierre is correct in his assumption, then *Turbulent* must have struck an underwater obstruction, in this case a mine, during daylight hours, as this is when submarines navigated submerged so as to avoid being sighted by enemy vessels and aircraft.

The following is an article written by Jean-Pierre for an unnamed newsletter on the subject of the wrecks he discovered with his sonar sweeps. The article is dated 26 January 2018.

For the Record
Tabarka, WWII Wrecks/Tombs

> A couple of persons have declared having doubts about the revelations of the sonar sweeps off Tabarka. They are apparently unable (or unwilling) to accept the reality revealed by sonar imagery. They only trust the archives that they consider Holy Scriptures. Their first problem is that no archive contains anything about these lost submarines; not a single survivor to tell the story, no witnesses (the shore is uninhabited to this date).
>
> Their second problem is that when a submarine disappears from the surface of the sea (contrary to the case of a big surface ship), it does not mean its wreck will be found on the seabed. If not totally

> disabled, if only damaged, a submarine, which is built to navigate under water, will try to get away from the theatre of the events and make its way back to its base.
>
> This occurred many times during the Second World War. In the case of the submarine wrecks off Tabarka, it appears that some of the vessels that are (soon?) to be identified, will prove to have been attacked elsewhere (by depth charging and even ramming), survived the attack and in trying to escape, stumbled blindly in to the uncharted minefield (at Tabarka) which appears to have been laid sometime in December 1942, most probably by the Italian 3rd Submarine Flotilla, who operated out of Bizerte (Tunisia).

It is important to point out that the minefield laid in the waters immediately off the coast of Tabarka, which it is claimed is the final resting place of *Turbulent* and several other British Royal navy submarines, was not just some hap-hazard placement. The mines were positioned across nautical traffic lanes known to be used by British vessels, particularly submarines, on a regular basis as they made their way between Malta, Gibraltar and Algiers. When leaving from or arriving at Algiers, submarines would have done so in a submerged state during daylight hours, and until they were ready to make for open waters they would have stayed relatively close to the shore line, meaning they would have been totally blind to a fully submerged enemy minefield, potentially sailing straight into it.

Another point about the minefield at Tabarka is that its presence does not appear to be that well documented in either

Italian or German archives or records. In fact, the only source for its existence is Jean-Pierre Misson. If he is correct, then the obvious question must be whether it is still there. If its location was unknown, then the chances are that the mines laid there were not cleared away after the war, which could prove problematic in any future exploration, especially as over time any such munitions would have become extremely unstable.

It is now recognised that during the Second World War, the Italian navy laid somewhere in the region of 55,000 mines throughout the Mediterranean. However, this fact was not widely known by the British authorities at the time, and one must consider how much more effective British submarines operating in the Mediterranean would have been if the true extent of the Italian and Axis minefields had been identified. Nevertheless, if the Axis nations had not lost so many ships, equipment, oil, military supplies and men to the efforts and bravery of the British submarines and their crews, the course of the North Africa campaign could have resulted in a completely different outcome.

Jean-Pierre's point about there not always being a direct correlation between where a submarine is spotted and attacked on the surface to where its eventual wreck is discovered on the seabed is a logical one, but it is not necessarily something that is initially considered when discussing such matters. He goes on to say that:

> Some people are not sufficiently open minded, and not sufficiently versed in the reading of sonar images, to accept evidence that contradicts "the established truth" (what is found in archives or published in books and other documents).

For the time being I will not react to the accusations of my revelations being "fantasies, imagination" or outright "hoaxes", but at some point in time these people will be brought to account, if not by me, surely by the souls resting in their steel tombs, on the seabed, off Tabarka.

It is very much hoped the British and Italian Naval Authorities will take steps to identify by name the six British submarines, and the one Italian submarine.

My main obligations have been fulfilled. I have disclosed to the British, Italian and Tunisian authorities what the sonar images show, along with the GPS co-ordinates of each wreck and the correlation of the sonar images with photographs of submarines known to have been operating in the area at the time they were lost.

What remains to be done is a proper, professional sonar plotting of all the wrecks in the area and then a conclusive identification of each submarine, by name. This is something beyond my capabilities and remains in the hands of the British, Italian and Tunisian authorities to take forward and act upon.

The misgivings of a couple of persons should not prevent this work from being done.

I hereby repeat my statement that there are six British submarines (including the *Turbulent*) off Tabarka. The immediate task would be to ascertain this claim by confirming the presence of one or

> two submarines, this would then in turn justify the launching of a full survey.

As already stated, it is not the intention here to attempt to endorse or verify Jean-Pierre's claims about what he discovered, but his claims certainly warrant further exploration.

Why would a man, who by his own admission is in the twilight years of his life, put his reputation at stake? Other than personal pride in a job well done, he has little to gain from the situation being clarified one way or another.

In February 2019 Jean-Pierre issued the following statement in relation to his sonar discovery (where the number of British submarines "discovered" has suddenly jumped from six in 2018 to eight):

STATEMENT OF IDENTIFICATION

> This is to confirm that one Italian and eight British submarines that vanished during WWII have been found on the bottom of a very limited speck of the Mediterranean Sea, off Tabarka, Tunisia.
>
> Each of these nine submarines is the tomb of its entire Crew.
>
> The Italian submarine is a CLASSE 600 boat, presumed to be of the Serie PERLA: the CORALLO (49 crew).
>
> The British submarines are, by order of disappearance:
>
> HMS TETRARCH, TALISMAN, TIGRIS, UTMOST, P. 222, THUNDERBOLT, TURBULENT, USURPER (Total crew 430 plus).

They were all lost between October 1941 and October 1943.

The wrecks of two surface vessels are found in the same area: Destroyer HMS Quentin and Schnellboot S.35.

All these wrecks have been identified from their sonar image alone, compared to vintage pictures, drawings and what information could be found on the Internet and in books concerning the whereabouts of the boats before they vanished.

The large amount of submarines can only be due to the existence there, during WWII, of an anti-submarine minefield.

Except to those who laid this obstruction, its existence and its exact position have remained unknown to all, until some sonar sweeps (2014-2015) very unexpectedly revealed what was on the seafloor.

A subsequent Visual Approach will only confirm that, for all the above cases, the Desk-Identification was correct and that:

A wreck can be identified from its sonar image alone, without necessarily a visual approach.

The mines of an anti-submarine barrage are moored in position by anchor-blocks, they are kept at some depth below the surface, they are not floating at the surface, they are not meant to sink a surface vessel.

Such a minefield is invisible and only effective against submarines navigating submerged (blind) and when a mine is made to explode the boat goes to the bottom in seconds, there is very rarely any survivor, there is rarely any significant debris, there is never any signal sent to base.

Despite their heavy losses, the British Submarine Service could never have pinpointed this minefield on the map because it is only less than half a square kilometre in dimension.

The Italian and British Embassies in Tunis were informed as to "some WWII submarines lying off Tabarka" in the fall of 2015.

The Tunisian MoD were informed in September 2016.

The minefield that existed there during the war has been located 3 nautical miles offshore, in position 37°04'N, and 8°52'E.

Because of the high loss of British submarines and because of the date of the first casualty, it is obvious the field was laid by the Italian Regia Marina. In that area, the sea floor rises to a plateau at about 65m, the distance from the shore and the depth of this location were ideal for the positioning of

> a submerged, anti-submarine obstruction. The alignment of the wrecks is indicative of the general orientation of the line of mines.
>
> Since this obstruction does not seem to be mentioned in official WWII archives and since it has remained unsuspected for three quarters of a century .... it is not known if the zone has been swept clean of the mines after the war.
>
> This Statement of Identification can be checked against the sonar recordings and the dossier of evidence for each wreck.
>
> The recordings have already been submitted to the Tunisian Marine Nationale (MOD, 14 September 2016) and to the Italian Marina Militare, who is intent on conducting a survey of the area in September this year.
>
> There has been no request from the British authorities for a copy of the recordings or for evidence of the identifications.
>
> Jean-Pierre Misson
> Brussels, 27 February 2019.

It is quite clear from Jean-Pierre's statement that this is a subject he feels extremely passionate about, although he is the first to admit that there are those who either openly dispute his claims or find them hard to accept. These aspects are not helped due to the lack of any targeted surveys having taken place to confirm or refute his sonar discoveries by either the Italian or British authorities. This lack of progression on the matter appears to be more to do with political wranglings with the Tunisian government rather than a lack of desire on the part of the Italian and British governments.

On 4 February 2019, Jean-Pierre received an e-mail from the British Defence attaché to Libya, who at the time was a serving officer in the Royal Navy. He was somewhat miffed by the comments and observations Jean-Pierre had made in relation to a lack of action and desire to identify the wrecks in the waters off Tabarka.

> Dear JP,
>
> Thank you for keeping me up to date with the various moves on this front.
>
> To be honest with you I am slightly saddened by the comment that we, the UK, "have not moved yet". The Royal Navy has five survey vessels. One is permanently attributed to Antarctica and our international obligations there; one is a deep ocean survey ship permanently attributed to the Atlantic and Indian Oceans (though, through defect has not been available recently. She is also fitted with sonars that would be entirely inappropriate in this case); one is a brand new inshore survey vessel permanently attributed to UK harbours and ports and the remaining two (ECHO and ENTERPRISE) have been committed to life-saving in the Mediterranean and English Channel (since 2014) when not completing NATO deployments to Ukraine in support of our

allies in the face of Russian aggression. The Royal Navy also has several international agreements to fulfil ranging from the Far East to the Caribbean; and the Falklands to northern Norway. Our global commitments make scheduling this work a challenge. Our ships and people are certainly not languishing at home with nothing to do.

We also, as I have mentioned before, do not have an agreement with Tunisia about surveying in their waters, and therefore cannot do anything legally until such time as that would be forthcoming. The UK takes this matter seriously and are delighted that Italy can spare the time and effort to survey this site in Sep 19. As a key ally and partner, Italy, a very professional hydrographic nation, is welcomed onto this task. I am confident that they will share their data widely so that further life can be breathed into this important task.

We have asked the Tunisian government for meetings on this topic but as yet they have not materialised. Our UK to Tunisia Defence relationship is growing and I am confident that in time this meeting request will be granted and then we can talk about possible ship commitment. I had hoped that our two ship visits in 2018 (by a Hydrographic ship fully capable of undertaking this task) would have spurred some action but this was not the case. I think you can see that we have "moved"; so it is a shame that you chose to make such comments to your wide following. Despite that I will persist, undeterred, in making this happen.

> To again be honest, it does sit lower down my schedule than our collective efforts on Counter-Terrorism on a day-to-day basis; honouring the dead is important, but so is protecting the living.

The last sentence of the e-mail is particularly poignant, especially the final two lines, "honouring the dead is important, but so is protecting the living". What appears to have been forgotten here is that the men who are entombed in these sunken vessels voluntarily and willingly served their country in a time of war. These were young men in their prime, who left their friends and families behind them to go to fight in a war hundreds of miles from home. In doing this they paid the ultimate price. The debt of gratitude that they and their families are owed can never be fully repaid. Protecting the living is very important, but finding the resting place of those who helped provide us with the very freedoms that we now enjoy, and whom many might take for granted, is a debt that we owe to the fallen and their families, and must not be forgotten.

The fact that seventy-six years after the end of the Second World War, the final resting place of hundreds of these lost souls has still not been discovered is not good enough. This is compounded even more when the location of a number of these wrecks is known, but regardless of the reasons why, we still do not know which vessels and the remains of which men are there.

On 18 March 2019, Jean-Pierre Misson sent an e-mail to an Italian researcher, who also had an interest not only in the wrecks discovered at Tabarka, but also the anti-submarine obstructions (minefields), which had been put in place to deter the passage of Allied submarines.

In the e-mail Jean-Pierre begins by pointing out that the first vessel to have struck one of the mines off Tabarka was the Royal Navy submarine HMS *Tetrarch*, which was "lost at the end of October 1941". This submarine, under the command of Lieutenant Commander George Henry Greenway, was not on a war patrol at the time it was lost but was on its way to America for a refit. Its journey had begun on 26 October 1941, when it had left Malta. Its intended route included pre-arranged stops at Gibraltar before heading to the UK, with its arrival at Gibraltar scheduled for 2 November 1941. It never arrived. As with all the other Royal Navy submarines that Jean-Pierre believes are to be found in the waters off Tabarka, its final resting place is yet to be officially confirmed.

There are similarities between the loss of *Tetrarch* and *Turbulent* in that at the end of the war patrol the latter was on when it went missing, it, too, was due to make its way to America for a refit.

An entry on the website www.uboat.net for HMS *Tetrarch* states that, "she is presumed lost on Italian mines off Cape Granditola, Sicily, Italy on 27 October 1941". Cape Granditola, incidentally, is approximately 275 miles away from Tabarka.

The Strait of Sicily is a stretch of water in the Mediterranean Sea, sitting between the island of Sicily and the Tunisian coast. The Strait was heavily mined by the Italian navy from as early as late August 1940, a tactic which certainly paid dividends for the Axis powers as over the following three years, a number of British submarines and surface vessels were lost there. Nevertheless, the Strait of Sicily is approximately 150 miles away from Tabarka.

Although the mines at Tabarka had more than likely been laid by Italian naval vessels of the Regia Navale, the mines were no doubt supplied by Germany, as the latter had established a mine warfare, research and development command as far back as 1920. During the Second World War it is estimated that German mines accounted for a total of 534 merchant vessels lost at sea. These mines were made from a combination of different elements, with aluminium accounting for nearly 40 percent of the mine's contents.

Further on in the e-mail, Jean-Pierre mentions the types of mines he believes were the ones used: "The mines must have been Moored Contact Mines (not Surface Mines), submerged because most of the wrecks (at Tabarka) are submarines, with very few surface vessels on the bottom."

Moored contact mines (*Elektrische Minen*) were electric mines set below the surface of the water at different depths, making them dangerous to surface vessels, such as aircraft carriers or large merchant vessels, whose hulls sat low in the water, and submarines alike. The design of these mines meant that they could be set at different and specific depths under the surface, specifically to target submarines. They could be set singularly or in groups at slightly different depths, thus potentially fatal for any submarine that found itself in their midst.

Whilst talking about the mines, Jean-Pierre further mentioned that: "It would appear the obstruction was of Italian origin because at the time it was laid the Germans were not yet very active in the Mediterranean and because the German Schnellboote only came to lay mines off the coast of Tunisia in the second half of 1942, at the earliest."

It must have been clear to the British naval authorities that they had a problem, but despite losing so many submarines across the Mediterranean Sea, it appears nobody at the Admiralty, or anywhere else for that matter connected with the British, made any kind of connection between the many submarine disappearances which had occurred in that area.

Jean-Pierre concluded his e-mail with the following observations:

> This Anti-Submarine obstruction came to be a major interference in British submarine movements throughout the Mediterranean, but without it being ever accurately "located" (so as to be avoided). Until the time when some sonar sweeps were conducted off Tabarka in 2014 and 2015 (and apparently to date) nobody had ever heard about these wrecks and what caused them to be all clustered there.

It is interesting to note that although the waters in the Strait of Sicily had been heavily mined by the Italians during the war, the same could not be said about the area off Tabarka, where Jean-Pierre's sonar scans were carried out in 2014 and 2015. "Because no trace of this mined obstruction has (yet) been found in Second World War archives and because it went unnoticed for so long, it is quite probable the area was never cleaned of its mines after the war."

What makes this scenario particularly scary is the suggestion that some of the mines laid at Tabarka might still be there. According to Jean-Pierre, no record to date has been found of the Italians having ever laid any mines in the area. The only saving grace today is that submarine movements there are probably non-existent, but it does not exclude the possibility that the same obstructions could still be a real and present danger for local fishermen who work those waters.

The following is an unpublished open letter written by Jean-Pierre in August 2019 to provide an update on his research. It was available for anyone who had contacted him regarding the story of HMS *Turbulent*'s disappearance.

To Whom It May Concern

It appears that, additionally to the Ministry of Defence, other Tunisian Ministries have now expressed interest in the WWII wrecks off Tabarka that I, Jean-Pierre Misson, fortuitously sonar-detected in 2014/2015, geo-located and then identified from documents, vintage pictures and constructional drawings.

All the research work and the results have been obtained through a desk study. There has been no diving of the wrecks for a visual approach, whatsoever.

The interest of various Ministries is encouraging news, but it comes with some demand for the confirmation of the discovery to remain undisclosed until they, the Tunisian authorities, decide how and when to release the information.

Note:

Following an agreement from the Tunisian Ministry of Defence, the Italian Navy will co-operate with the Tunisian Marine Nationale to survey the zone off Tabarka, where J P Misson claims there is one British destroyer, HMS *Quentin*; one German E-boat, S. 35; one Italian submarine, the *Serie Sirena*; eight British submarines, HMS *Tetrarch*, *Talisman*, *Utmost*, *P 222*, *Tigris*, *Thunderbolt*, *Turbulent* and *Usurper*.

A cargo ship, slightly outside the zone, has remained unidentified. There are many more wrecks in that area, 600 x 200m, presumed to have been an anti-submarine obstruction during WWII.

Remarks:

Under International Law, all naval vessels (found as wrecks) remain under sovereignty of the flag nation, therefore all these wrecks are still the property of Great Britain and Germany. There are no Tunisian casualties inside any of these wrecks. All nine submarines are the tomb of their entire crew. There are 444 British and 45 Italian nationals inside these submarines. There were no survivors.

All 489 submariners have been missing for three quarters of a century, without anyone knowing where they were, since the day they disappeared. Only the sonar sweeps revealed the submarines, hence their final resting place.

Their families have been waiting for such a long time to know their whereabouts that for delaying for one minute the release of this information would amount to a blatant violation of human rights.

In my position of discovery of these souls it is my duty and obligation to tell the families where their loved ones really are, and I strongly object to delaying the release of the information as to where they are, because surely the Tunisian authorities will allow the members of these families to come to the site to honour them with some remembrance service out at sea.

> The legal department of the Tunisian Ministry of Foreign Affairs will certainly confirm all of the above and it is regretted that this Ministry did not get involved in this matter from the very beginning as they surely know better than any other Ministry the various international laws relevant to this case.
>
> To summarise, I would hope the results of the forthcoming joint Italian – Tunisian investigation on the identity of the wrecks off Tabarka, particularly the identity of the submarines (War Graves) will be disclosed, if not to the public, at least the families, as this is a legal as well as a moral obligation.
>
> Jean-Pierre Misson
> Tabarka, 1 August 2019.

To date, more than three years later, the joint investigation by the Italian and Tunisian authorities, which Jean-Pierre mentions above, has still not taken place, with no obvious reason or clear explanation as to why this is so.

On 31 August 2019, Jean-Pierre e-mailed the defence attaché at the British Embassy in Tripoli, Libya:

> Dear Sirs,
>
> Further to some earlier exchanges on the subject, I wish to summarise the situation as follows:
>
> It seems CV Fantoni has encountered difficulties in the last stage of negotiations with the Tunisian authorities. I do not have the details but it appears

> some Ministries (other than Defence) worry about the risk of these wrecks being "looted" should their presence and position be revealed. In my view this is an attempt to delay (possibly postpone indefinitely) the survey of the area which was supposed to be conducted by a vessel of the Italian Navy during the period 2-13 September 2019.

No such survey was carried out by the Italian Navy by September 2019, nor has a subsequent survey been carried out as recently as January 2022.

> Their objective was to SONAR-GPS plot all the wrecks (revealed by my five sonar sorties of 2014-2015) so as to mark them on the charts with accuracy (they are not a danger to surface navigation but certainly are a danger to fishing trawlers). The other immediate goal would have been to identify by name their one submarine, which is a "Classe 600" boat, most probably the SMERALDO.
>
> They were also to try and identify the non-Italian wrecks, i.e.; the destroyer HMS QUENTIN and the eight British submarines that I say are; HMS TETRARCH, TALISMAN, UTMOST, P 222, TIGRIS, THUNDERBOLT, TURBULENT, and USURPER.

Jean-Pierre's e-mail was accompanied by a number of attachments, including maps of the region showing where he claims the sunken wrecks are located.

The task of identifying British submarines by name is difficult and can only be performed by the Royal Navy. A British survey is needed. It would not be advisable, nor proper, to rely on others to do this job.

Considering there are eight British submarines + destroyer HMS QUENTIN in a limited perimeter of 600 x 200m, it would certainly be appropriate for the British Naval Authorities to come over and confirm my revelations because the eight boats are war graves (with the remains of 444 British submariners), and their families have not been officially told yet of where they are resting.

Considering the superior weight of the British wrecks and casualties in that speck of sea off Tabarka, it is obvious the British Authorities should confirm the revelations I have submitted to the British Embassy in Tunis as early as the Fall of 2015 and which I continuously updated to this date.

I have repeatedly offered to justify my claims with comprehensive presentation of my research work and the evidence that the sonar imagery correlates with the vintage pictures and the constructional drawings of the submarines and of the destroyer HMS QUENTIN.

My offer still stands, wherever I may be asked to do such a presentation.

> As far as a survey of the seafloor off Tabarka is concerned, and irrespective of the outcome of the Italian investigation, I feel it is ample time the British authorities take some action of their own, without relying on others.
>
> To avoid lengthy negotiations at Ministerial level, a British envoy could go straight to the Tunisian Head of State because this case of "444 missing British nationals" would certainly justify an approach at this level.
>
> The pre-requisite to any such action is for the British Embassy to be convinced of the reality of what lies on the sea floor off Tabarka.
>
> I am not sure this is so and therefore I remain available to remedy the case.

Jean-Pierre did not have to wait too long for his reply. Four days later, he received the following email from the defence attaché at the British Embassy in Tripoli:

> Dear Jean-Pierre,
>
> Thank you as ever for your e-mails. Sadly I am not surprised at the difficulties encountered by Paolo, having dealt with similar issues over the past 3 decades as a professional mariner and hydrographic surveyor, this is entirely normal. As we discussed previously, even when we found a wreck of an RN

vessel from WW2 (sunk by mine action) outside a particular state's 12 nautical mile territorial water limit we (the UK) have been legally unable to publish the information. This is because the wreck lay within 200 nautical miles of the nation state in question and they have, to date (after 4 years of effort) not conceded to release the information. And that was after we had gathered it. It took 3 years to get to a point of data collection. The UK does like to follow the law; even where this is inconvenient.

As discussed last time, I have discussed this subject at length with Navy Command in the UK and the Royal Navy Historical Branch and the Geographic Managers at the UK Hydrographic Office in Taunton, and all are on side. The elections here in Tunisia are effectively shutting down all non-normal activities with the Tunisian government; but we will persist on all avenues as previously advised. [Name (1), Name (2), Name (3), Name (4)] and I, are all in contact and discuss this routinely, trying to navigate a clear way through.

[Name (2)] and I are refining our diaries and hope to come to visit you and discuss in great detail your findings within the next 10 days. When would be best for you?

My new Ambassador arrives tomorrow and I am committed to a number of events next week that follow up from the UN SRSG's briefing to the

Security Council this afternoon (on the Libya conflict), but I am determined to make something work. [Name (2)] also has a few external visits to juggle.

Many thanks for your persistence.
Yours.

It was clear from the wording of the e-mail that Jean-Pierre's claims were being taking reasonably seriously, and were certainly not being ignored.

Two hours later, Jean-Pierre replied.

Dear [Name (5)],

Thank you very much for your mail which I regard as some promise of action.

I will be in Tabarka until Saturday 28th but would prefer a much earlier date for your visit.

This matter of telling the families where exactly 444 British and 45 Italian submariners are resting cannot be dropped. My first approach of the Tunisian authorities was at Foreign Affairs level, through the Tunisian Ambassador in Madrid.

Not only because it is this Ministry who will be the first beneficiary of the sonar revelations but because this case comes under International Conventions (Wrecks of Warships and War Graves).

CV Fantoni apparently omitted to involve the Tunisian Ministry of Foreign Affairs because if he had done so, the Italian Authorities (Navy) would have certainly obtained permission to send a Survey Ship, not after three years of negotiations but probably after three months.

It is the Tunisian Ministry of Foreign Affairs that knows about International Conventions, not the Ministry of Defence (or any other Tunisian Ministry, for that matter).

I had been told the Italian Navy's Investigation would be conducted by a Survey Ship, 2 to 13 September 2019.

I have received no further news on this plan. I understand some other Tunisian Ministries have now joined the discussions between the Ministry of Defence and Italian Navy, to demand that the results of the Investigation be withheld. This is unacceptable to the Families that have been waiting so long to know the true location of their loved ones.

In my view, the only way out of this (apparent) deadlock is for the British to be convinced they have eight submarines and 444 submariners, lying on the sea floor off Tabarka (the Italians seem already convinced they have one submarine there with 45 crew).

Once the British and the Italian Ambassadors would be convinced of that, then I see no better way of obtaining permission to despatch a Survey Ship (to confirm all the sonar revelations 2014 - 2015), than a joint British - Italian move at Diplomatic Level.

I have been to the Commando Marittimo Sicilia, Augusta, Sicily, in March 2018 and gave the evidence I have about one of the wrecks being a WWII Italian Classe 600 submarine (presumably the SMERALDO).

I have had no similar opportunity to brief in full any British Official, yet, despite my constant emailing (as early as the Fall of 2015) of the results of my study of the sonar recordings, with the identification of eight British submarines and one destroyer BY NAME.

The results have been arrived at by correlating the sonar image of a wreck to the vintage pictures and the drawings we have of these vessels. None of these wrecks has been dived.

Looking forward to your visit I remain, dear [Rank & name]

Yours sincerely
Jean-Pierre Misson.

It is interesting to read these e-mails to and from Jean-Pierre because regardless of what the truth is, and no matter what the authorities from the different nations involved really thought of him and his claims, they were certainly prepared to engage with him. At the same time there were certain individuals on military history forums who not only questioned his claims, but who were quick to ridicule and almost vilify him for what he was saying, when all he had done was to claim that the wrecks of certain vessels were in a particular location in the Mediterranean, and then pushed the Tunisian, Italian and British authorities to carry out underwater surveys of the location he has identified. Why anybody in the circumstances would be so sceptical, is unclear.

Jean-Pierre's images were captured whilst using a sonar Starfish 450, made and produced by Tritech Ltd., a company who specialise in advanced underwater sonar technology and who are "dedicated to providing the most reliable imaging and ancillary equipment for use in underwater applications". His identifications of the wrecks have been arrived at by compensating the rather low definition of the sonar images with thousands of hours of scrutiny to correlate the sonar image to the vintage pictures and constructional drawings of the vessels he claims are there.

He claims if an identification is possible from low-grade definition sonar images, then this means that with sonar images of a higher definition, the identifications of the wrecked vessels can be confirmed or corrected, particularly as all the basic work has already been done and the vintage documents are in hand.

A survey of the area where Jean-Pierre claims to have identified and located the wrecks, which is only 600 x 200m, would, by his estimation, only require about one hour of sonar-sweeping at the most.

Part of Jean-Pierre's attempts at convincing the British authorities of what he found included emailing Navy Command on four separate occasions in January 2020. He received a reply in a letter dated 25 March 2020.

Dear Mr Misson,

(1). Further to your e-mails of 7, 10, 11 and 24 January 2020 regarding the wrecks off the coast of Tabarka, Tunisia, I have received advice from our subject matter experts. My understanding is that you believe that you have achieved positive identification of wrecks through use of limited sonar imagery and documentary research. Further to that you believe that the wrecks in the proximity of Tarbarka include:

- HMS QUENTIN (G 78),
- Schnellboot S 35,
- Eight British submarines and;
- One Italian submarine.

(2). Regarding your idea that sonar imagery alone should be accepted as a means of positively identifying a wreck, it is agreed that it is a possibility, but it depends on the characteristics of the wreck, the quality of the sonar recording and the number of independent sonar records. The Ministry of Defence (MOD) would not make such a judgement on single images where the sonar may not have been set up or deployed correctly; in such instances a good sonar can still return an image but that any imagery gained this way is of dubious utility. Consequently, the images may not be conclusive, and open to different interpretations. It is agreed that conventional photography alone is unlikely to be the sole means of identifying many wrecks. A combination of historical records and high-resolution sonar scans and imagery is considered by the MOD to be the most likely means of positively identifying most wrecks.

(3). Your e-mail of 10 January 2020 contains an attachment titled 'TABARKA Chronology of Losses APR 2019'. However, contemporary records and investigations, suggest the following.

a. HMS TALISMAN: Assumed post war to have been mined and sunk in the Sicilian Channel on 17 September 1942.

b. HMS TIGRIS: A documentary investigation carried out in 1986 provided strong evidence that the TIGRIS was sunk on 27 February 1943, by the German A/S vessel UJ 2210 to the south of Capri.

c. HMS TURBULENT: An exhaustive documentary investigation carried out in 1994 concluded that HMS TURBULENT was mined and sunk off the east coast of Sardinia between 14 and 18 March 1943.

d. HMS UTMOST: Assumed post war to have been sunk by the Italian Torpedo Boat, GROPPO to the north west of Marettimo, west of Sicily, on 25 November 1942.

e. HMS P.222: Assumed post war to have been sunk by the Italian Torpedo Boat FORTUNALE south east of Capri on 12 December 1942.

f. HMS TETRARCH: Presumed mined off Cap Granitola, Sicily.

g. HMS THUNDERBOLT: Presumed sunk off Cap St. Vito, Italy.

h. HMS USURPER: Presumed to have sunk in the Gulf of Genoa.

(4). While only HMS P48 is believed to have been sunk off the coast of Tunisia, it was in the vicinity of the north west of Zembra Island, which is a significant distance away from Tabarka. Those submarines which had been ordered to patrol off the Italian coast were subsequently lost and are presumed to be off the Italian coast. The MOD recognises the lack of absolute certainty over the exact location of all the vessels listed above. However, for so many of these units to be so far from where they were deployed to, would be very unusual, but it is conceded that this is not completely impossible.

It is the very uncertainty and confusion over where the MOD believe all these vessels actually are and where Jean-Pierre is suggesting they are, that is the reason why further investigation to clarify the matter is urgently required. It is clear from the MOD's response that at present they do not know where any of the vessels are located, but Jean-Pierre's sonar scans strongly suggest that he has at least found something that is worth further investigation. Such intervention will not only clarify the matter one way or another, but it will clear up, once and for all, exactly what Jean-Pierre Misson has found at Tabarka.

> (5). In conclusion, in the absence of indisputable evidence (high resolution sonar and imagery), the MOD is unable to support your belief that you have identified these specific wrecks. Should new evidence such as high-resolution imagery and sonar images taken after 2019 be forthcoming, the MOD would be keen to consider that evidence, but not resubmissions or reconstructions of current imagery.
>
> (6). It is appreciated that this reply may be very disappointing, especially as it is unlikely that further independent surveys or explorations can be made off the coast of Tabarka for some time. Our Defence relationships in Tunisia are concentrated on countering the contemporary threats from terrorism and violent extremism. We do continue to explore other opportunities to deepen the UK-Tunisia Defence relationship and will endeavour to keep you informed should survey opportunities be forthcoming in the future.

Although quite clearly not want Jean-Pierre was hoping for, the Royal Navy's balanced and honest response was prepared to recognise certain aspects of what he had put forward. But despite this, the truth will only ever be discovered when the wrecks at Tabarka can be fully and properly inspected, so that each of these submarines can at last be identified. As a nation we surely owe it to the memories of the brave men who are entombed inside them, and to their relatives, to once and for all know discover where their final resting place is.

On 10 December 2021, the author e-mailed Jean-Pierre to enquire if the intended joint Italian and Tunisian survey which had been due to take place in September 2019 had taken place. On 11 December, he received the following explanation:

> They cancelled the mission after the Tunisians objected to the use of anything more (Sonar, ROV, Divers) than conventional Depth Sounder, and after the representative of the Institute National du Patrimoine (INP), (they have an Underwater Research division), expressed concern that the public revelation of the existence of WW2 wrecks would expose these wrecks to looting by unscrupulous divers.
>
> Italian Navy Officers had come over to Tunisia to negotiate the programme of work, [whilst] Tunisian Navy officers had gone to Italy to finalise the Accord, yet it all went astray because of some apparent interference/jealousy between Tunisian Ministries.
>
> I tried to find out whether the mission had only been postponed to a yet undetermined date, or cancelled altogether. Apparently it was postponed because of continuous Covid worries in Tunisia, and because of the very unstable political situation (many Ministerial changes) in the country. The mission has not yet been re-activated.
>
> I still have contact with the current Italian Defence Attaché in Tunis, a Navy officer, the third DA I have dealt with since I first reported my findings to the Italian Embassy in Tunis back in 2015.

> I went to see the British Defence Attaché(s) in Tunis, in September 2019, where I gave a three-hour-long briefing with a display of documents on a screen.
>
> The Royal Navy Captain who had previously been the British Defence Attaché had completed his tenure and been replaced by a Colonel from the British Army.
>
> The British are understandably not so enthusiastic about confirming the wrecks of so many of their submarines and their destroyer HMS *Quentin*, having been lost in a place that to date, they knew nothing about.
>
> Unless there is a change of attitude and unless someone admits to the families of the many British ratings lying there (they deserve to be told where their loved ones are), I do not believe there will ever be an investigation carried out by the British Ministry of Defence into the wrecks that I believe exist in the waters off Tabarka.

This reply appears to highlight the current lack of desire on all sides to want to take this matter further.

The author sent Jean-Pierre a further e-mail on 14 December 2021, concerning the potential route HMS *Turbulent* would have taken on its way back to Algiers at the end of its last war patrol:

> Having looked at a document from the British National Archives, which had originally been marked as "Most Secret", the official line appears

> to have been that *Turbulent* was more than likely sunk by a mine off Maddalena sometime on or after 14 March 1943. Even if that was not the case, and the submarine continued her journey down the east coast of Sardinia to then make her way to her base at Algiers, once she had reached the tip of Sardinia, she would have had no reason to go anywhere near Tabarka. So my question to you is, what makes you so certain that the wreck of HMS *Turbulent* is to be found in the waters off of Tabarka?

Jean-Pierre's reply was as follows:

> Whether coming back from Maddalena or Capri, any submarine returning to Gibraltar or Algiers would always make a landfall on the coast of North Africa, then crawl along coming to periscope depth every 20 minutes or so, to take fixes on conspicuous landmarks, so as to obviate the need to bring the much too visible Conning Tower to the surface, and allow the Navigator to get on the [dry] bridge for astronomical fixes on the sun. This was simply too dangerous to do and placed the *Turbulent* at risk of being sighted by enemy aircraft.
>
> The *Turbulent* would have remained fully submerged during daylight hours. Being submerged they were "blind" and could not see the undetectable anti-submarine mines very cleverly placed across the sea-lanes running between Gibraltar-Malta, near Tabarka.

> The sonar images I captured revealed the fairing of a (reversed) Torpedo Tube No. 10. There was only one T-Class submarine operating in the area at that time, Group 3, with reversed Torpedo Tube No's 9 and 10. This submarine was HMS *Turbulent*.

It is now nearing seventy-seven years since the end of the Second World War. Those who have it in their power to find out the truth about what Jean-Pierre Misson discovered in the waters off Tabarka have a moral obligation to the memory of those who lost their lives there and to clarify once and for all what happened to HMS *Turbulent* and the other Allied vessels lost at sea.

Conclusion

The stark reality is that nobody knows with any degree of certainty what happened to HM Submarine *Turbulent* and its crew after it disappeared in early 1943.

What is known is that the vessel left its base in Algiers on 24 February after an eleven-day break, having returned from its eleventh war patrol on 12 February and filling up with sufficient fuel, food, water, and ammunition before leaving. John Deller re-joined the crew after having been treated in hospital, whilst his good friend, George Svenson, had to leave the ship with jaundice, an act which undoubtedly saved his life.

Turbulent's orders were to focus its patrol in the Tyrrhenian Sea, which is surrounded by the west coast of Italy, the French island of Corsica to the north, Sardinia to the west and Sicily to the south. It is accessible to the north by the Ligurian Sea, the Mediterranean Sea to the west and Ionian Sea to the south, and has a surface area of 106,200 square miles. At its deepest point it measures 12,418 feet, so it would not be difficult for a vessel to get lost within its confines, below the surface or above the waves.

The 865-ton Italian merchant vessel the *San Vincenzo* was attacked with torpedoes and gunfire before being sunk on 1 March 1943, off Paola, Italy. The vessel believed to have carried out the attack was HMS *Turbulent*, but it should be noted that there is no solid evidence to support that suggestion.

The reality of how HMS *Turbulent* met its end can, I believe, be sensibly discussed in three ways; it either struck a mine, was sunk by an enemy vessel, or struck an underwater object with such force that the propeller broke, leaving the submarine immobilised on the sea floor.

Suggestions put forward as to how *Turbulent* was lost include that it struck a mine off Maddalena in early March 1943, or that it was attacked and sunk by the Italian torpedo boat the *Ardito* off Punta Licosa on 6 March 1943. There was also the suggestion that on 12 March 1943, *Turbulent* was sunk by depth charges dropped from an anti-submarine vessel.

As early as June 1940, Royal Navy submarines of the Mediterranean Fleet, which was operating out of Alexandria, had started to become victims of enemy tactics in the Mediterranean Sea. In just a matter of days in June 1940, the submarines *Odin, Grampus* and *Opheus* were sunk, although not one of them was sunk by a mine. Two were sunk by Italian destroyers and the other by Italian torpedo boats, highlighting just how effective the Italian navy were.

Within a couple of months, the Italians had changed tactics and had decided on a strategy of mining the Mediterranean in an attempt to reduce the effectiveness of the Royal Navy. They particularly targeted the Strait of Sicily, which runs between Sicily and the coast of Tunisia, and is 145 kilometres in width and just over 300 metres at its deepest point. It also separates the Tyrrhenian Sea from that of the western Mediterranean.

As an example of the confusion and uncertainty surrounding the loss of HMS *Turbulent*, and how its disappearance was not an isolated incident, during the months of November and December 1940, two Royal Navy submarines, HMS *Regulus* and *Triton*, were both lost, but it is still unknown exactly how either of them met their demise. The discussion centres around whether they struck mines or were sunk by enemy vessels or aircraft, exactly the same discussions which still exist about *Turbulent* and its disappearance over two years later.

Between 1940 and 1943, the issue of whether a vessel had been lost after having struck a mine appears to have been a common topic of conversation. If any losses could not be confirmed or fully explained, it was assumed a mine was to blame. This was certainly the case with *Turbulent*. What makes their eventual discovery and identification all the more difficult is that because it is not known precisely on which date they were lost, it is harder to work out exactly where the wreckage may be. As discussed previously, the 76-year-old amateur Belgian diver Jean-Pierre Misson claims to have discovered the wrecks of a number of Second World War submarines on the seabed, off the coast of Tabarka in Tunisia. One of these he believes to be the wreck of HMS *Turbulent*.

HM Submarine *Turbulent* had been in service for less than two years when it went missing on 23 March 1943, on what was its twelfth and final war patrol. Regardless of the mystery surrounding its disappearance, the skill and abilities of the man who commanded it was ultimately what made the difference between how successful it was. In the case of *Turbulent*, John Linton was its one and only commanding officer. The partnership of Linton and *Turbulent* resulted in the sinking of twenty-four enemy vessels, not to mention a further six attacks that were launched but proved to be unsuccessful.

One question that will always remain unanswered in relation to *Turbulent* is whether it would have been remembered and spoken about in so much detail if it had not been involved in the infamous attack on the *Nino Bixio.* It is hard to say for certain, but the chances are it would simply have been one of the many submarines lost in mysterious circumstances during the Second World War.

APPENDIX A

Crew of HMS *Turbulent* in March 1943

At the time of its loss on 23 March 1943, there were a total of sixty-seven officers and ratings on board HMS *Turbulent.* No bodies were ever recovered. Despite the men dying together, their names are commemorated on three different naval memorials at Chatham, Plymouth and Portsmouth.

Twenty-eight of the men either received a military award or were mentioned in despatches; a remarkable achievement for the crew of just one submarine.

Baker, Lieutenant Arthur Osmond
Bennett, Able Seaman Frederick George Newhouse
Biddlecombe, Leading Seaman William Henry Joseph
Billingsley, Able Seaman Morgan Ensor
Blake, Lieutenant John Priestley (DSC)
Bourne, Stoker 1st Class Albert Edward
Boyce, Stoker 1st Class James Michael
Boyce, Stoker 1st Class Victor Cornwall
Brokenshire, Able Seaman Henry

Bromby, Chief Engine Room Artificer Harry (DSM)
Brown, Telegraphist Norman
Chartres, Lieutenant (E) Clive Frederick Evelyn
Clements, Lieutenant Brian Clement Weston (DSC)
Courtnall, Leading Stoker Cyril Frank
Crowston, Engine Room Artificer 3rd Class Arthur Stanley (DSM) & Bar
Darling, Stoker 1st Class Cecil (MiD)
Deller, Able Seaman John Albert
Dennis, Leading Telegraphist Ronald Arthur
Down, Stoker 1st Class Cyril Stanley Thomas
Dye, Stoker 1st Class Walter James (MiD)
Farrow, Leading Seaman William Edward
Ford, Able Seaman Cyril Davis
Gardner, Petty Officer Cook (S) Tom (DSM)
Glester, Able Seaman William Arthur (DSM) (MiD)
Glover, Able Seaman William Henry
Goldsworthy, Stoker 2nd Class Andrew
Gorman, Telegraphist Bernard
Hadley, Chief Petty Officer Telegraphist William Kerly (DSM)
Hall, Stoker 1st Class Richard
Hay, Stoker 1st Class George
Hogg, Petty Officer William (DSM)
Hunnisett, Able Seaman Brian
Jones, Able Seaman Norman Edwin
Linton, Commander John Wallace (VC DSO DSC)
Lloyd, Petty Officer Stoker Christopher Albert (MiD)
Lyfield, Chief Petty Officer Albert Ray (MiD)
Mason, Engine Room Artificer 4th Class George Leonard
Maynard, Leading Stoker Albert Ernest
Morris, Able Seaman Cyril Edward
Morris, Electrical Artificer 1st Class Frederick Charles (DSM)

Oates, Leading Seaman Leonard Charles
Ogden, Able Seaman Charles
Ormerod, Able Seaman Maurice
Pearce, Leading Seaman Charles Henry (MiD)
Peebles, Yeoman of Signals William Carton (MiD)
Reeves, Able Seaman Robert Herbert (DSM) (MiD)
Richardson, Leading Telegraphist William (DSM)
Ridley, Able Seaman Robert Rowcroft (MiD)
Sharp, Petty Officer Stoker William Edward (DSM)
Simpson, Engine Room Artificer Malcolm (MiD)
Stead, Able Seaman John (MiD)
Stone, Able Seaman Frederick Percival de Main (DSM)
Stranaghan, Leading Stoker Harold (MiD)
Sweeney, Stoker 1st Class Joseph
Todd, Leading Stoker Charles Alfred
Tunnell, Stoker 1st Class Joseph William Thomas
Walker, Petty Officer Henry Frederick (DSM)
Wallis, Engine Room Artificer 4th Class Frederick Charles (DSM)
Walton, Able Seaman Leslie
Weatherley, Petty Officer Steward James William
Wheeler, Leading Stoker Frank Thomas
Wheldon, Able Seaman Harold Walter
Whyte, Engine Room Artificer 4th Class Hugh McLaren
Wilkes, Chief Petty Officer George Harold (DSM)
Williams, Able Seaman Geoffrey Alwyn
Willicombe, Stoker 1st Class Thomas John (DSM)

APPENDIX B

New Zealand Soldiers Killed in the Attack on the *Nino Bixio* by HMS *Turbulent*

The following list contains the names of 116 New Zealand soldiers known to have been killed when the Italian cargo ship *Nino Bixio* was struck and damaged by torpedoes fired by the Royal Navy submarine HMS *Turbulent* on 17 August 1942.

The list appears in the book, *No Honour, No Glory*, by Spence Edge and Jim Henderson (1983), although the names are also included on the Commonwealth War Graves Commission website. It is important to remember that the men had been divided alphabetically between the *Nino Bixio* and the *Sestriere.*

The men are commemorated on the Alamein Memorial in Egypt. Nineteen bodies were recovered and were initially buried at the Jalova Military Cemetery in Greece, before being moved and re-buried at the Phaleron War Cemetery in Athens.

Chell, Private 66808 Ernald Freeman
De La Mare, Signalman 31876 Ivar Charles
Lang, Private 29676 Herbert
Le Bailly, Private 64235 Henri William
Lee, Private 45822 Allan Henry
Lusk, Private 17316 Edward Albert
MacKintosh, Private 15521 William Winder
MacPherson, Private 62519 Peter Marryatt
Maguire, Private 62104 John Terence
Major, Private 37188 Herbert Lester
Mangos, Private 46136 George Gordon Drummond
Marsh, Private 65553 Charles
Marshall, Private 24173 James Lawrence
May, Private 65125 Frank Henry George
McAlpine, Private 26261 John/James Duncan
McConachy, Private 35498 John
McCracken, Private 36894 Leo George
McDonald, Private 26494 Donald
McIntyre, Private 5838 Thomas Malcolm
McKenzie, Private 65000 Alexander
McKenzie, Sergeant 14409 Donald McFarlane
McLachlan, Private 32529 William Douglas
McLean, Private 63997 James
McLellan, Private 18940 John Grierson
McLeod, Private 45876 George Allan
McNamara, Private 29599 John
McQuoid, Private 12327 Alfred Lionel
Miller, Private 28205 Lloyd Lindsey
Moores, Sergeant 38568 David Albert James
Moorhead, Private 24186 Winton Lester
Morrice, Private 24188 William
Morris, Lance Corporal 44364 Ernest George

Neal, Private 67234 Dene Lawrence
Needham, Gunner 16464 William Herbert
Neilsen, Private 34150 Keith Bredahl
Nicholson, Corporal 37261 John Andrew
Notman, Private 24207 Archibald John Forbes
Page, Private 44477 Gordon
Palmer, Private 19482 Walter Vernon
Pamplin, Private 64424 William Richard
Papps, Private 30918 Kenneth Weston
Parsons, Private 29419 John Alfred
Paton, Private 46928 Glen Forbes
Patterson, Private 46928 Albert John
Pavici, Private 33695 Ivan George
Peters, Private 60115 Raymond Leslie
Peterson, Private 19635 Douglas
Pharazyn, Private 4138 David Robert
Piper, Private 13683 Joseph
Player, Corporal 24236 Douglas Henry
Plummer, Private 12329 George Henry
Poi, Private 24238 Kalika
Polhill, Private 13698 Frederick William
Potts, Private 15129 James Oswald
Rand, Private 42544 Verdun Clifford
Randle, Private 25341 Patrick
Reader, Private 3237 Leonard Douglas
Reid, Private 14146 Noel Henderson
Rendall, Gunner 22365 James David
Ripley, Corporal 63856 Ronald Arthur
Robertson, Lance Corporal 14095 Charles Maslin
Robertson, Private 66985 Eric Campbell
Robertson, Private 35319 John Fletcher
Robinson, Private 35206 Albert John

Rogers, Private 63395 Patrick Noel
Rowe, Private 46191 Oscar Trimble
Sampson, Private 45430 Basil Claude
Sargisson, Private 44012 Alfred Francis
Schmidt (Smith), Private 24300 Leonard George
Seymour, Private 33602 Charles
Sherry, Private 40256 John Francis
Simpson, Corporal 26157 James George
Skinner, Private 62367 Howard Martin
Small, Private 132295 Herbert Leslie
Smith, Private 48113 John Urban
Smith, Private 24300 Leonard George (real surname Schmidt, but served as Smith)
Speake, Private 37143 Horace
Stanley, Private 45330 Douglas Earl
Stantiall, Private 45845 Clarence Arthur
Stanton, Private 65102 Reuben Jerome
Stead, Private 46140 Arthur Robert
Steed, Private 66504 George
Stevenson, Private 19032 David Robert
Stewart, Private 44444 Alfred Henry John
Sutherland, Private 18809 Norman Lindsay
Swan, Lance Sergeant 35720 Peter
Symes, Private 64161 Tui Vincent
Taylor, Private 12392 Gordon Norrie
Taylor, Private 31753 James Michael
Telford, Sergeant 31686 John Myles
Theyers, Private 33434 Walter Alexander
Thompson, Private 65110 Ashley Aubin
Thomson, Corporal 24332 Frederick Hugh
Thomson, Private 14579 Kenneth William James
Tibbles, Private 44550 Donald Arthur

Tonks, Private 15363 John Robert
Tooth, Private 24336 Donald Charles
Trevella, Private 15188 Charles James
Truman, Private 45852 Lawrence Noel
Tucker, Gunner 22325 John
Tudhope, Gunner 22376 Thomas William McFarlane
Wakelin, Private 64110 Leo Oliver
Wares, Corporal 17516 Owen
Watt, Private 45270 Douglas John
Watts, Private 24361 Grahame Falconer
Watts, Private 45920 Raymond Harold
Wedge, Private 19805 Neil Richard
Wells, Private 12595 David Robert
Whalley, Private 14615 Benjamin
White, Private 23005 James
White, Signalman 31854 William Glen
Wilde, Gunner 16233 Eric
Wilson, Private 67089 Lancelot Fenwick
Wilson, Private 64127 Norman William
Wilson, Private 67144 Robert Henry
Windle, Private 13960 William Henry
Woisin, Lance Corporal 24385 Vernon Carl

The following New Zealand men are also believed to have been victims of the attack on the *Nino Bixio* but are not shown as having died on 17 August 1942. Instead, it is believed they subsequently died of their wounds sustained in the initial attack.

18 August 1942

Gorton, Private 5800 George Joseph William
Swale, Serjeant 13294 Andrew McLeod

19 August 1942

Dunn, Private 11574 George Owen
McKay, Private 24149 Norman Roderick

20 August 1942

Sola, Private 26557 Wilfred Gregory

21 August 1942

Budd, Second Lieutenant 4964 Brian Hastings
Wallace, Private 33746 Wilbert Harwood
Watson, Lance Serjeant 20947 Roland Henry

22 August 1942

Lang, Private 63824 George Godfrey
Taylor, Private 44549 Percy Edward

23 August 1942

Van Dyke, Private 24351 Ernest Malcolm

It would appear that although New Zealand forces are shown as having lost 116 men in the initial attack on the *Nino Bixio*, during the eight days immediately afterwards at least eleven more men subsequently died from injuries and wounds sustained in the event.

APPENDIX C

Australian Soldiers Killed in the Attack on the *Nino Bixio* by HMS *Turbulent*

The following list contains the names of forty-one Australian soldiers known to have been killed when the Italian cargo ship *Nino Bixio* was struck and damaged by torpedoes fired by the Royal Naval submarine HMS *Turbulent*, on 17 August 1942.

Once again, the Allied POWs who were placed on board the *Nino Bixio* were, in the main, men whose surnames began with initials J through to Z.

Their names are commemorated on the Alamein Memorial in Egypt.

Johnstone, Private VX41848 Frank Arnold
Jones, Flight Sergeant 404635 Edward Austin
Lavercombe, Private QX8089 Anthony
Lewis, Private WX9616 Maurice Willian
Male, Private WX11972 Archie Graham

Maslen, Private WX8987 Daniel Mannix Patrick
Maslin, Corporal WX5372 Selwyn Frank
Mason, Corporal WX8372 Herbert Ernest
Maunsell, Private WX13593 Shamus Joseph Edgar
McBeath, Private QX5953 Leslie Norman
McDonald, Flight Sergeant 400351 Kenneth Stewart
McGrade, Private WX6549 Ernest Leo
McKenzie, Private WX5581 Andrew
McMeekin, Private WX9106 Norman Francis
McNess, Private WX6004 Norman Hurtle
McPherson, Private WX13178 Charles
Merritt, Private WX5910 Edward Collin
Miller, Private WX7013 Harold Kiffen
Moir, Corporal WX11442 Ross Newland
Morgan, Private NX51424 Keith
Morris, Private WX9435 Albert Henry
Morris, Private WX9424 William Arthur
Mullane, Private WX8627 Malcolm Saunders
Mullane, Private WX4960 Richard Mervyn
Murphy, Private WX5914 Edward John
Neilsen, Private WX4903 Hugh Clifford
Nuttall, Private WX14822 Ronald
Osborne, Private WX13496 John
Osborne, Private WX5719 John Thomas
Page, Gunner NX33447 Keith Harrison
Parker, Private WX3840 Richard
Paterson, Private WX14827 George
Paterson, Private WX7016 James Laidlaw
Patterson, Sergeant NX 10075 Robert John
Price, Private WX7979 John Alfred
Price, Private WX5294 William Victor

Prosser, Private WX202 Matthew Clarence
Richards, Private WX8721 Peter
Roden, Gunner NX27353 Alexander
Tancred, Private QX8806 John Fairfax
Thompson, Private WX14416 Thomas Herbert

APPENDIX D

British Soldiers Killed (or Believed Killed) in the Attack on the *Nino Bixio* by HMS *Turbulent*

The records of the Commonwealth War Graves show that the following men served with the British Army during the Second World War and died on 17 August 1942, with no known grave. Unless otherwise stated, their names are commemorated on the Alamein Memorial in Egypt, strongly suggesting that they were lost at sea.

The infantry regiments in which these men served all saw action during the North African campaign prior to the date of the attack on the *Nino Bixio.* While it cannot be confirmed that these men were killed in the attack, it is surely a great coincidence that they died at sea on the exact same day the *Nino Bixo* came under fire.

Adamson, Signalman 2343445 Thomas. 10th Indian Divisional Signals, Royal Corps of Signals
Allan, Serjeant 4339745 George Henry Mayne. 1st Battalion, Kings Own Royal Regiment (Lancaster)

Blackburn, Private 3597936 Joseph. Border Regiment

Coppack, Lance Corporal 3524974 Albert. 1st Battalion, Lancashire Fusiliers

Davies, Corporal 3657586 Ernest. 1st Battalion, Kings Own Royal Regiment (Lancaster)

Dean, Private 5437224 Allen Albert. 1st Battalion, Duke of Cornwall's Light Infantry

Hackett, Signalman 2344026 William Gordon. 10th Indian Divisional Signals, Royal Corps of Signals

Hardy, Serjeant 2032502 George Henry. 1st Battalion, The Queen's Royal Regiment (West Surrey)

Hartley, Private 3715291 Thomas. 1st Battalion, Kings Own Royal Regiment (Lancaster)

Haugh, Corporal 3777782 John Vincent. 1st Battalion, Kings Own Royal Regiment (Lancaster)

Heron, Private 7358334 John Patrick. 9th Light Field Ambulance, Royal Army Medical Corps

Hurdman, Signalman 2361235 Richard Charles. 10th Indian Divisional Signals, Royal Corps of Signals

Lamb, Private 371594 Alfred. 1st Battalion, Kings Own Royal Regiment (Lancaster)

Lowe, Private 3710770 Joseph Walters. 1st Battalion, Kings Own Royal Regiment (Lancaster)

MacNamara, Serjeant 1585065 Bernard Joseph. Royal Artillery

Maidwell Private 5826172 Leonard. 1st Battalion, Kings Own Royal Regiment (Lancaster)

Manbridge, Corporal 5437184 Stanley Frederick. Duke of Cornwall's Light Infantry

Martin, Private 10553572 Eric Stanley. 5th Ordnance Store Company, Royal Army Ordnance Corps

McAndrew, Private 7371721 Anthony William. 62nd General Hospital, Royal Army Medical Corps

McNeil, Private 3711182 William. 1st Battalion, Kings Own Royal Regiment (Lancaster)
Meakins, Private 4919612 James. 9th Battalion, Durham Light Infantry
Middleton, Private 7377906 John. 9th Light Field Ambulance, Royal Army Medical Corps
Millson, Signalman 2369066 Leonard. 10th Indian Divisional Signals, Royal Corps of Signals
Mimms, Private 4346164 Sidney. 5th Battalion, East Yorkshire Regiment
Moody, Private 4458150 William. 8th Battalion, Durham Light Infantry
Morley, Corporal 5882015 George William. Northamptonshire Regiment. (Attached) 10th Indian Division, Provost Unit
Murphy, Lance Corporal 7917489 Albert Desmond. 50th Royal Tank Regiment, RAC
Nix, Corporal 5884155 Stanley Harold. Northamptonshire Regiment. (Attached) 10th Indian Division, Provost Unit
Nottage, Driver T/276615 George Leonard. Royal Army Service Corps. (Attached) Royal Army Medical Corps
Patefield, Trooper 7941731 Norman Birch. 50th Royal Tank Regiment, RAC
Petersen, Private 7345240 Victor Arthur. 149th Field Ambulance, Royal Army Medical Corps
Peterson, Private 4348060 Harry. 5th Battalion, East Yorkshire Regiment
Pickthall, Trooper 7941496 Leonard. 50th Royal Tank Regiment
Presgrave, Driver T/232498 Frank. Royal Army Service Corps
Rowney, Trooper 7904798 George Wilfred. 42nd (23rd Battalion, The London Regiment), Royal Tank Regiment, RAC

Russell, Private 3715376 George. 1st Battalion, Kings Own Royal Regiment (Lancaster)
Sclare, Gunner 992624 David. Royal Artillery (Attached) 10th Indian Division
Spence, Fusilier 6980482 Robert Lloyd. 2nd Battalion, Royal Inniskilling, Fusiliers
Spooner, Gunner 863088 Joseph. 1st Field Regiment, Royal Artillery
Stevens, Lance Serjeant 7917140 William George. 'A' Squadron, 40th (7th Battalion, The Kings Regiment [Liverpool])
Sweeney, Private 3241315 Edward. 1st Battalion, Kings Own Royal Regiment (Lancaster)
Tholander, 2nd Lieutenant 200777 Cecil Joseph, 5th Battalion, East Yorkshire Regiment, attached from the West Yorkshire Regiment
Torevell, Lance Corporal 3777242 William. 1st Battalion, Kings Own Royal Regiment (Lancaster)
Tubb, Private 6094261 Frank Hutton. 1st Battalion, Sherwood Foresters (Notts and Derby regiment)
Turner, Serjeant 4457355 Clifford Landreth. 9th Battalion, Durham Light Infantry
Turner, Lance Corporal 3709285 William Edward. 1st Battalion, Kings Own Royal Regiment (Lancaster)
Uttley, Gunner 1090183 Ernest. 124th Field Artillery, Royal Artillery
Waterman, Lance Corporal 5334938 Charles Frederick. Royal Berkshire Regiment. (Attached) 10th Indian Divisional Provost Unit
Watson, Lance Corporal T/73119 Jack Joseph. Royal Army Service Corps. (Attached) 9th Light Field Ambulance, Royal Army Medical Corps

Wheeler, Trooper 7919787 Maurice Henry. Royal Tank Regiment, RAC. 40th (7th Battalion, The Kings Regiment [Liverpool])
Wilson, Trooper 7890678 William Robert. Royal Tank Regiment, RAC. 40th (7th Battalion, The Kings Regiment [Liverpool])

Phaleron War Cemetery

The Phaleron War Cemetery is situated on the outskirts of Athens in Greece. After it was damaged during the attack by HMS *Turbulent*, the *Nino Bixio* was towed across the Mediterranean Sea to the Greek port of Pylos.

Eleven members of the British Army who died on board the *Nino Bixio* are now buried at the Phaleron War Cemetery.

Martin, Private 4346264 William. 5th Battalion, East Yorkshire Regiment
Mills, Private 4618109 Maurice Samuel. 5th Battalion, East Yorkshire Regiment
Morgan, Private 4466532 Patrick 8th Battalion, Durham Light Infantry
Mottram, Trooper 7904051 W.F. 7th Battalion, Royal Tank Regiment, (Liverpool) RAC
Muir, Private 7366678 James Crawford. Royal Army Medical Corps
Murray, Private 4346342 James. 5th Battalion, East Yorkshire Regiment
Peel, Private 4461386 Roger Walter 8th Battalion, Durham Light Infantry
Prosser, Gunner 941950 Joseph James. 11th (Honourable Artillery Co.) Regiment, Royal Horse Artillery

Riley, Serjeant 7894001 John Edward. 50th Royal Tank Regiment, RAC

Sherratt, Trooper 7933092 William F. 50th Royal Tank Regiment, RAC

Thompson, Trooper 7917570 Norman John. 50th Royal Tank Regiment, RAC

APPENDIX E

Indian Soldiers Killed (or Believed Killed) in the Attack on the *Nino Bixio* by HMS *Turbulent*

The following Indian soldiers died of their wounds, or were killed in action, on 17 August 1942 following the attack on the *Nino Bixio* by HMS *Turbulent.* Their names are commemorated on the Alamein Memorial in Egypt.

Ali, Lance Daffadar 6770, Mumtaz. 'A' Squadron, Prince Albert Victor's Own Cavalry (11th FF), IAC
Bhosle, Sepoy 9407 Baliram. 2nd Battalion, 5th Mahratta Light Infantry
Gul, Sepoy MTN/511825 Spin. 21st IBT Company, Royal Indian Army Service Corps.
Gurung, Rifleman 37071 Birkha Bahadur. 2nd Battalion, 3rd Queen Alexandra's Own Gurkha Rifles
Illahi, Cook 04072 Fazl. 10th Indian Divisional Signals
Juman, Sweeper F/741488. 25th Indian Infantry Brigade, Transport Company, Royal Indian Army Service Corps

Kadam, Naik 171 Kashiram. 2nd Battalion, 5th Mahratta Light Infantry

Khan, Sepoy 20314 Adam. 4th Battalion, 13th Frontier Force Rifles

Khan, Sowar 9069 Aziz Muhammad. Prince Albert Victor's Own Cavalry (11th FF) IAC

Khan, Sapper E/12740 Khalil. 7th Artisan Works Company, Indian Engineers

Khan, Signalman A/5324 Lal. 10th Indian Divisional Signals, Indian Signal Corps

Khan, Gunner 46529 Muhammad. 1st Anti-Tank Regiment, Royal Indian Artillery

Masi, Mess Cook F/1138 Budhu. King George V's Own Bengal Sappers and Miners

Rangnekar Sepoy 13646 Laxuman. 3rd Battalion, 5th Mahratta Light Infantry

Shripati, Naik 9417 Bhogaode. 2nd Battalion, 5th Mahratta Light Infantry

Singh, Sapper 12507K Atma. 41st Field Company, Indian Engineers

Singh, Sepoy MT/914632 Durga. 25th Indian Infantry Brigade, Transport Company, Royal Indian Army Service Corps

Singh, Cook F/741715 Hardayal. 25th Indian Infantry Brigade, Transport Company, Royal Indian Army Service Corps

Singh, Sapper 23759 Ishar. King George V's Own Bengal Sappers and Miners

Singh, Sepoy MT/895068 Kartar. 25th Indian Infantry Brigade Transport Company, Royal Indian Army Service Company

Singh, Sepoy MT/902573 Kartar. 25th Indian Infantry Brigade, Transport Company, Royal Indian Army Service Corps

Singh, Sapper 23261 Mohan. King George V's Own Bengal Sappers and Miners

Singh, Sapper 21559 Narayan. King George V's Own Bengal Sappers and Miners
Singh, Sepoy 16328 Nikka. 4th Battalion, 11th Sikh Regiment
Singh, Sapper 21963 Pal. King George V's Own Bengal Sappers and Miners
Singh, Sapper 12052/K Panjab. King George V's Own Bengal Sappers and Miners
Singh, Barber MT/741107 Raunaq. 25th Indian Infantry Brigade, Transport Company, Royal Indian Army Service Corps
Singh, Sapper 22730 Sarjit. King George V's Own Bengal Sappers and Miners
Singh, Fitter ME/45293 Sundar. Indian Army Ordnance Corps, (Attached) 25th Indian Infantry Brigade
Wadhawa, Sepoy MTN/913709, 25th Indian Infantry Brigade, Transport Company, Royal Indian Army Service Corps

Twelve further Indian soldiers are recorded by the Commonwealth War Graves Commission as having died on 18 August 1942, and are also commemorated on the Alamein Memorial. It is possible that these men were also lost when the *Nino Bixio* was attacked, but their loss was not confirmed until the following day.

Bhagowalia, Jemader TY/1392 Sher Muhammad. 179th Supply Personnel Section, Royal Indian Army Service Corps
Das, Sepoy 22789 Ganesh. 4th Battalion, 10th Baluch Regiment
Khan, Sapper 22754 Akram. 107th Railway Operating Company, Indian Engineers
Lakshmanan, Sapper 16502, 10th Field Company, Queen Victoria's Own Madras Sappers and Miners
Singh, Gunner 46889 Atma. 2nd Anti-Tank Battery, 1st Anti-Tank Regiment, Royal Indian Artillery

Singh, Driver 46169 Bachan. Royal Indian Artillery

Singh, Gunner 47485 Balbir. 2nd Anti-Tank Battery, 1st Anti-Tank Regiment, Royal Indian Artillery

Singh, Naik 13644 Gurbakhsh. 2nd Battalion, 11th Sikh Regiment

Singh, Sepoy 12400 Karam. 2nd Battalion, 11th Sikh Regiment

Singh, Sowar 11852 Puran. 2nd Royal Lancers, IAC

Singh, Driver 46270 Rachan. 3rd Indian Anti-Tank Battery, 1st Anti-Tank Regiment, Royal Indian Artillery

Yellayya, Sapper 17290, 10th Field Company, Queen Victoria's Own Madras Sappers and Miners

APPENDIX F

South African Soldiers Killed (or Believed Killed) in the Attack on the *Nino Bixio* by HMS *Turbulent*

The following South African soldiers were all killed, or died, on 17 August 1942, and are listed as such by the Commonwealth War Graves Commission. Because of the locations where they are buried or the memorials they are named on, they can be reasonably assumed to have been casualties from the attack on the *Nino Bixio* by HMS *Turbulent.* They are all commemorated on the Alamein Memorial unless otherwise stated.

Badiroang, Private N/13320 A.S. Native Military Corps (Fayid War Cemetery, Egypt)
Beckman, Lance Bombardier 105542 K.W. 1st Field Regiment, South African Artillery
Kirsten, Lance Corporal 241692 Phillip. 1st Battalion, Rand Light Infantry

Lawrence, Private 2678 A.R. 2nd Battalion, Royal Durban Light Infantry
Seaton, Corporal 10441 R.C. St., Die Middelandse Regiment. (Phaleron War Cemetery)
Senfftleben, Lance Corporal 186121 H.T. South African Medical Corps
Wade, Bombardier 90582 L.F. South African Artillery

Sources

Ancestry.co.uk
1911 Wales Census
www.myweather2.com
www.cwgc.org
www.uboat.net
Submarine Service Movement Record Index Card
British Newspaper Archive
www.cityofaley.com
www.wrecksite.eu
www.naval-history.net
www.wartimememoriesproject.com
www.britannica.com
www.nzhistory.govt.nz
www.history.navy.mil/library/online/sub_turtle.htm
Submarines (1977) Richard Garrett
Human exploration of the deep: Fifty years and the inspiration continues (2009) William Kohnen
www.theworldwar.org
www.jstor.org
The Second London Naval Treaty

www.anzacpow.com
www.campo57.com
www.hansard.parliament.uk
www.nationalarchives.gov.uk
www.findagrave.com
www.awm.gov.au
www.surname.rootschat.com

About the Author

Stephen is a happily retired police officer having served with Essex Police as a constable for thirty years between 1983 and 2013. He is married to Tanya, who is also his best friend.

Both his sons, Luke and Ross, were members of the armed forces, collectively serving five tours of Afghanistan between 2008 and 2013. Both were injured on their first tour. This led to Stephen's first book *Two Sons in a Warzone – Afghanistan: The True Story of a Fathers Conflict*, which was published in October 2010.

Both of Stephen's grandfathers served in and survived the First World War, one with the Royal Irish Rifles, the other in the Mercantile Navy, whilst his father was a member of the Royal Army Ordinance Corp during and after the Second World War.

Stephen corroborated with one of his writing partners, Ken Porter, on a previous book published in August 2012, *German POW Camp 266 – Langdon Hills*. They have also collaborated on four books in the 'Towns & Cities in the Great War' series by Pen and Sword.

Stephen has co-written three crime thrillers which were published between 2010 and 2012, and centre round a fictional detective named Terry Danvers.

When he is not writing, Stephen and Tanya enjoy the simplicity of going out for a morning coffee, lunch time meals or walking their four German shepherd dogs early each morning, whilst most sensible people are still fast asleep in their beds.

Other works for Pen & Sword include:

The Surrender of Singapore: Three Years of Hell 1942-45 (2017)
Against All Odds: Walter Tull, the Black Lieutenant (2018)
Animals in the Great War (2018) (co-written with Tanya Wynn)
A History of the Royal Hospital Chelsea – 1682-2017: The Warriors' Repose (2019) (co-written with Tanya Wynn)
Disaster before D-Day: Unravelling the Tragedy of Slapton Sands (2019)
Countering Hitler's Spies - British Military Intelligence 1940-1945 (2020)
Mystery of Missing Flight F-BELV (2020)
Holocaust: The Nazis' Wartime Jewish Atrocities (2020)
Churchill's Flawed Decisions: Errors in Office of the Greatest Britain (2020)
The Lancastria Tragedy: Sinking and Cover-up 1940 (2020)
The Shetland 'Bus': Transporting Secret Agents Across the North Sea (2021)
Dunkirk and the Aftermath (2021)
St Nazaire Raid, 1942 (2022)
The Blackout Ripper: A Serial Killer in London, 1942 (2022)

The author would like to say a particular thank you to the following individuals for allowing the use of photographs, images and written materials they were kind enough to share during the writing of this book.

Yvette Benson, John Deller, Jean-Pierre Misson,
Tony Rudd, Gordon Watkins and Gerald Norton-Knight.

Index